PERCEPTION AND CHANGE
Projections for Survival

Other books by John Platt

The Excitement of Science
New Views of the Nature of Man
The Step to Man

PERCEPTION
AND
CHANGE

Projections for Survival

———

Essays by
J OHN P LATT

Ann Arbor

THE UNIVERSITY OF MICHIGAN PRESS

For permission to reprint previously published material, grateful acknowledgment is made to the following sources.

The University of Chicago Press for "Diversity" from *The Knowledge Most Worth Having* edited by Wayne C. Booth, © 1967 by The University of Chicago; and for "The Two Faces of Perception" from *Changing Perspectives on Man* edited by Ben Rothblatt, © 1968 by The University of Chicago.

"The Limits of Reductionism" is reprinted by permission of the publishers from Everett Mendelsohn, editor, *Journal of the History of Biology*, Spring, 1969. Cambridge, Mass. The Belknap Press of Harvard University Press. Copyright, 1969, by the President and Fellows of Harvard College. (Originally published as "Commentary.")

The Dorsey Press for "Beauty, Pattern and Change" from *Functions of Varied Experience* edited by Donald W. Fiske and Salvatore R. Maddi.

"Communication and Collective Choice" is adapted from "Perception, Communication and the Future" in *33rd Conference Proceedings of the Educational Records Bureau*.

"Shaping the Evolutionary Future" is reprinted from *The Great Ideas Today 1968* edited by Otto Bird. Copyright © Encyclopedia Britannica Inc., 1968. (Originally entitled "The New Biology and the Shaping of the Future.")

"What We Must Do" is reprinted from *Science*, Vol. 166, pp. 1115–1121 (November 28, 1969.) Copyright 1969 by the American Association for the Advancement of Science.

To the children

Contents

SEEING

I

Diversity

More diversity in our science, our patterns of living, and our education would enrich us all.

I CELEBRATE diversity. Our research, our lives, our goals, our pursuit of excellence are all too homogeneous. La Rochefoucauld writes: "God has put as differing talents in man as trees in Nature: and each talent, like each tree, has its own special character and aspect. . . . The finest pear tree in the world cannot produce the most ordinary apple, and the most splendid talent cannot duplicate the effect of the homeliest skill."

I think he means that other men are not like him in being able to produce maxims of this kind. But what he says is true. How many of us have gotten D's and F's in apple-tree courses simply because the teacher was too narrow to see that we had to be nurtured as pear trees? Progress would be faster and life would be more interesting if we pursued more diverse goals—goals of excellence to be sure, but goals of our own, different from what everybody else is pursuing—and if we tolerated and encouraged the same sort of individuality in others. I want life to be various. I want to see around me not only apple trees but pear trees, not only fruit trees but slow-growing oaks and evergreen pines and rosebushes and bitter but salubrious herbs and casual dandelions and good old spreadout grass. Let us be different, and enjoy the differences!

THE SCIENTIFIC BANDWAGON

Nowhere are we as diverse as we might be. Science and technology today encompass thousands of specializations, yet it is easy to see that the specialists are probably overconcentrating on certain subjects while other subjects, of equal interest and importance and ripeness for development, are almost entirely neglected. A short time ago it was announced that there were over 400 government

3

and industrial contracts and projects for studying the optical laser, the device which is able to produce a peculiarly coherent and brilliant beam of light. Now this is an interesting field, but—400 projects! This represents several thousand scientists and engineers who have jumped, or been pushed, onto this bandwagon in the decade since the laser was invented. The motorcar was developed with less than 40 manufacturing and development teams, and the whole field of atomic spectroscopy was developed in perhaps no more than 40 research laboratories. One cannot help wondering whether everything important to discover in the field of lasers might not have been discovered just as fast with only 40 projects, with the other 360 groups doing something less repetitive. One suspects that many of the 400 projects might not have been started if their leaders had known in advance—before they got their grant money and could not back out—that they would be competing with 399 others.

Over the past 25 years I have changed my own field from physics and chemistry to biology, and I think that, in every field of science I have seen, there are areas that are being overstudied in this way by men who might be doing something more valuable with their brains. There is not only bandwagoning, there is nitpicking, where a multiplying succession of scientists pursues more and more ingrown exercises in what were originally interesting and important subjects. I am polite and will not name all these areas. That is left as an exercise for the student. But I think there may be symptoms of overstudy in some parts of molecular chemistry, where even the insiders often admit that they are doing rather repetitive studies on rather repetitive series of molecules. And some nuclear physicists, in relaxed moments, will be heard to sigh that the research teams are too big and the apparatus too complicated and the results hardly worth the effort any more. Many physicists have changed to molecular biology, where there seems to be more novelty and more scope for individual creative achievement. But in that field also there are now complaints that too many hundreds have taken up "the DNA game" and that it is time to move on.

Many of the men in these areas will defend their studies, of course. They have ego-involvement, as they should have; and financial dependence as well. If there are many men in a subject, they can point quite accurately to many achievements, and can say quite truthfully that with more men and more money they would have had even more. The important thing they do not say is what other, perhaps more valuable, things they might have done instead. Perhaps only the broad administrator, or the student not yet committed, has the detachment to make a real comparison of this kind, judging the promise of different fields and their excess study or neglect.

One reason why some fields are overstudied these days is our present system of government grants. If the grand old man in a certain field was skilled in "grantsmanship" just after World War II and got large grants or contracts for a few years, he was able to feed numerous undergraduate and graduate and postdoctoral students. As a result, within a few years he produced a dozen more trained scientists in the same field, specialists who had published papers and who knew how to apply for grants and who, as established experts, would recommend each other's grants and might even become agency officials. And, from these trained scientists, a new generation of students has of course multiplied again, and international conferences must be held in this area of rapidly growing importance. It is a chain reaction. Even the undergraduates can see how important the subject is, with all those visiting lecturers passing through and praising each other.

Meanwhile, that poor old area where the senior scientist lagged in applying for his first grant a few years ago is still trying to catch up, but is falling farther and farther behind in money and manpower, regardless of its importance or equal promise of success.

I am exaggerating slightly, of course. Students do change subjects, and new discoveries are made which open up new fields. But the tendency is clear, and some fields will be overstudied and others will be neglected, as long as government granting agencies refuse to make value judgments between areas, and say, in effect, that whatever many scientists want to do—that is, whatever they were supported for learning to do as students 20 years ago—must be the thing most worth doing and worth supporting.

I think there are thousands of scientists who would like to change to less crowded and more interesting fields if they thought the move would not be disapproved and if they could see how to make a living and how to get research support while making the change. I think such moves would be a good thing. Mobility spreads the skills in a labor market, and mobility would spread the skills in science. Kant, Helmholtz, Pasteur, all changed fields. Enrico Fermi once said that a scientist should change fields every 10 years; that, in the first place, his ideas were exhausted by then, and he owed it to the younger men in the field to let them advance; and that, in the second place, his ideas might still be of great value in bringing a fresh viewpoint to a different field. If government agencies do not want to point the finger at some areas as being over-crowded, they might at least consider giving wide publicity to the relative numbers of men and projects in different areas and to the ranking of the importance or promise of these areas by experts from nearby fields; and they might be able to take the lead in pointing out *under*studied fields and in soliciting grant applications in such fields.

UNDERSTUDIED FIELDS

Are there understudied fields? There certainly are, and interesting ones too. In the field of the colors of molecular compounds, in which I have done some work, there must be hundreds of scientists studying the spectra of diatomic gases for NASA and the Air Force, and thousands of scientists studying the spectra of benzenes and petroleum compounds and dyes for the oil and dye and photographic industries, but only one or two laboratories have made systematic studies of the spectra of the flower pigments, and I have been able to find only one paper in English on the absorption spectra of the irises of our own eyes. These subjects are difficult, but no more so than many others which are avidly pursued, and they are of considerable biological and genetic and human interest.

Much of the work on visual pigments and on the biochemistry of vision was done in a single laboratory, that of George Wald at Harvard. And, in spite of the journalistic excitement that was produced a few years ago by the curious color demonstrations of Edwin Land of the Polaroid Corporation, the number of scientists working on the physics and chemistry and anatomy of color perception, or indeed of any aspect of perception, is still only a handful. The molecular basis of memory—what molecules are involved in the growth of nervous connections between brain cells when we learn something—is the subject of articles in the *New York Times* every week or two, but there are scarcely more than a dozen laboratories where such studies are being pursued. And the mechanisms of photosynthesis, in spite of their human and biological and economic importance for feeding the world, are probably being studied seriously at no more than about 20 laboratories, and the subject is still almost untouched by the powerful methods of the DNA revolution.

Marine biology—the problem of understanding the odd creatures of the sea and their development and cycles and diseases—is something done at only a few centers on the coasts, although the number is growing. But its importance for the life of the world should make it a matter for basic study by the best physicists, chemists, and biologists everywhere. I once heard the president of a Midwest university say that this was not a proper subject for emphasis at an inland school—even though his astronomers were working in both hemispheres, his cosmic-ray men had networks around the world, and his engineers were readying apparatus for solar system orbits from what is now Cape Kennedy. He was not "inland" except to marine biology.

In a more technical direction, we badly need new tools of research that almost no one is working on. In 1960 a theoretical study put forward that it might be possible to make improved electron microscopes that would permit one to see individual atoms or to identify a molecule directly just by looking at it. The importance of this for organic chemistry or biology may be imagined. It might be as great as the importance of the original electron microscope. But the number of qualified investigators who have applied for grants to try to develop such improved microscopes can be counted on the fingers of one hand. The development of research tools is not a traditional business of biology as it is of physics, and this and many other types of tools—such as new types of centrifuge, new methods of sectioning and staining and visualizing tissues, new methods for automating genetic studies—have often lagged because of the lack of scientists who will turn aside to develop them and the inability of our laboratories to assign task forces to these important projects, as they could easily do if it were a matter of military or space studies.

Some of the scientists who have been studying the design of automatic vehicles for the scientific exploration of the surface of Mars have hoped that such a vehicle would require the development of a completely automated chemical and biological laboratory for analyzing small samples of material. Chemistry and biochemistry have lagged behind other fields in applying computers and automation methods to laboratory analysis and synthesis. Students still pour liquids back and forth by hand and sit watching flasks boil, as they did in the time of the alchemists. An automated lab might change all this, with incalculable consequences in making our chemical and biochemical studies faster and simpler and more accurate.

In many fields of science there are lags and understudied subjects, just because of the narrowness of training in the fields themselves. In astronomy, many of the great developments of the last century have come from outside the field, including the analysis of ionization in stellar atmospheres; the hypothesis of nuclear reactions in the stars; radioastronomy; astrochemistry; magnetohydrodynamics; and the discovery of synchrotron radiation. Astronomers have tended to be ingrown, trained only by other astronomers and isolated away from the flux of new ideas in physics and chemistry, and they have often resisted such innovations.

Similarly, in medicine, many of the most fundamental advances have been made, not by doctors, but by physicists and chemists and biochemists. Witness the germ theory, the development of many antibiotics, and the DNA story, not to mention technical tools like x-rays and other radiation, the electron microscope, and radioactive tracers. There are exceptions, but all too often the training of young medical research men is a training in repetition rather than in the important new methods and ideas of biology and the other sciences. As one wit has said, "We learn exactly what we are taught. Send a man to jail for four years and he becomes a trained criminal. Send him to medical school for four years and he becomes self-important and incurious." It is an overstatement, but it has a core of truth.

Outside the sciences, philosophy is another field which is too ingrown. It suffers from being taught by philosophers. Many of the major new philosophical ideas of the last hundred years—creative evolution, pragmatism, empiricism, logical positivism, personalism —have come not from philosophy but from the sciences, biology, psychology, mathematics, and physics. Diversity, diversity! There are probably many other areas which I have not mentioned where the narrowness of training by the professionals is evidently an actual handicap to progress in the field.

On the technological side, we develop some things well and other things not at all. We send men into orbit and we can fly faster than sound, but our clothes are inferior to those of a bird in many ways. The technical design of clothes is still prehistoric, in spite of synthetic fibers and sewing machines. The fibers must still be drawn out like animal or plant fibers, then spun, then woven or knitted, and then cut and sewn more or less to fit, just as fibers and cloth have been spun and sewn for thousands of years. And then these threads do not protect us against rain or cold, or ventilate or shade us in the hot sun, unless we put on and take off many layers, which we must carry around in a suitcase. Why should someone not make us a single suit that would shed rain and that we could ruffle up for comfort in any weather, as a bird ruffles its feathers? A bird needs no suitcase. The reason is that no one—not even the Army, which might be expected to have the greatest interest in it—has put a task force on the problem of designing clothing material of variable porosity and variable thermal conductivity that could be molded to the body. Not everybody would want a single universal suit, but it would be nice to have the option. It might not even be very hard to invent. But we still have prehistoric patterns of thought in what touches us most closely. Helicopters, *si;* clothes, *no.*

It is the same story with shoes, which are still sewn of pieces of leather or plastic. And again with housing, which lags far behind automobiles in technology and still has piece-by-piece assembly and leaking roofs and windows and no standard modular connection to the needed city services.

It is as though we had collective taboos against certain types of development, like the taboo against work on oral contraceptives before about 1950, or the refusal to consider or finance Buckminster Fuller's geodesic dome buildings until the Army used the principle for radomes, or the reluctance of psychologists and physiologists to study sleep before the work of Nathaniel Kleitman and his coworkers made it respectable. Scientists are not really innovators, and neither are industrial companies and government agencies and their research-and-development teams. They all shrink, like other men, from unheard-of projects for which there is no precedent, even obvious and important projects, because they are afraid they will be laughed at or cut off from support.

As psychologists once backed away from the study of sleep, so biologists and doctors today back away from the study of regeneration and rejuvenation, although the central importance of these studies to human welfare is obvious. Such studies sound too much like science fiction—as though every development today did not!—and they have often been given a bad name by sensational reports like those of the "monkey gland" studies of the 1920's. But lower animals can regenerate parts of their bodies. Lobsters can regenerate claws; and newts, which are vertebrates much farther up the scale, can still regenerate eyes and optic nerves. It would seem that the power to do this is not lost in the higher animals but is only "turned off" or economized somehow, since we still have the full information for our embryological development preserved in every cell of our adult bodies. A concentrated study of "tissue inducers" or of the restoration of embryonic biochemistry might permit a useful measure of regeneration, and the discovery of how to do it might take only a fraction of the biologist-years now being spent on minor studies of DNA. A man who had lost a finger or a hand might find it very useful to grow, not merely skin over the stump, but bones and muscles, even if it took just as long as growing the original finger or hand. But we will never know whether it can be done until a few dozen scientists get to work on it.

So it is also with rejuvenation, or the preservation or restoration of sexual activity and enjoyment and of other youthful functions after the age of 50 or so. About 20 percent of the people of the world are in this age group, so this is a problem affecting the health and marital happiness of more than 600 million people. Some of the processes of aging that cause us to run down may be programmed innately into our genetic apparatus, while others may be due simply to the breakdown of certain repair mechanisms. Could these genetic programs be reversed or delayed? Or could the repair mechanisms be replaced? We do not know, but there are many avenues to try, and it seems to me quite possible that the work of a few hundred biologists in this important area might do more for the daily happiness of hundreds of millions of people than even a successful solution of the terrible problems of cancer and heart disease; yet the number of researchers in this field is probably not 1 percent of the number in the cancer field. We are driven by the fear of death, not by an interest in living more abundantly. Who would have the courage and love of humanity to try to organize an American Rejuvenation Society as rich as the American Cancer Society for the support of research? The jokesters would have a field day. And so the important thing does not get done.

There are other possible experiments that use the same biological principles and that would be extremely interesting to try, even though they are still more "far out." Since the nucleus of every adult cell in the body contains all the genetic information necessary for copying the complete adult, could we not take out some of these nuclei with a micropipette and insert one of them in a fertilized egg cell in place of the egg's own nucleus, letting the egg cell then develop and grow up into an identical twin of the original adult?

J. B. Gurdon of Oxford has already succeeded in doing this with frogs. If this procedure will work for higher animals, it could be the basis of a new animal-copying industry. One can imagine cells being taken from a prize cow or from a champion racehorse, and the nuclei from them being transplanted into newly fertilized egg cells and the egg cells reimplanted into a foster mother or into several foster mothers, producing several calves or foals which would all be identical twins of the champion. It could be a very profitable business! And it would be the fastest method of breeding enough superb stock for the developing countries.

For human beings, successful development of this method offers the possibility of giving babies to many couples who are unable to have children—babies which in this case could be genetic copies of the husband or wife. Many would find such a method infinitely preferable to our present method of artificial insemination from anonymous donors, with its genetic risks, or our method of adoption of babies from anonymous parents. And perhaps someday many mothers might want to try bringing up new copies of some of the great individuals of the world—great actors or athletes or musicians or thinkers or statesmen. Identical twins of this kind, reared in different homes, might enable us to find out for the first time how much of human achievement is due to heredity and how much to environment. If the genetic component is the determining factor, then in 25 years we might have the most remarkable collection of violinists or scientists or educators in the world!

It would also be useful to try animal-copying with the nucleus taken from one species and the egg in which it was implanted taken from another. Donkey and horse can be mated; will a donkey nucleus in a horse egg cell give a donkey—or something more like a mule? This might teach us something about the developmental embryonic differences between species. If it would work, we might be able to save some vanishing species by transplanting their cell nuclei into the egg cells of foster species. Is the DNA that carries heredity destroyed immediately when an animal dies? If the meat of woolly mammoths locked for thousands of years in the Arctic ice is still edible, perhaps their DNA is still viable and might be injected, say, into elephant egg cells to give baby mammoths again. By some such methods, perhaps we might achieve "paleo-reconstruction" of the ancient Mexican corn, or of "mummy wheat," or even of the flies that are sometimes found preserved in amber. One man has devoted his life to reconstructing creatures like the ancient aurochs, by backcrossing modern cattle. May not these other genetic methods of paleostudy also be worth trying? Success is uncertain, but the rewards would be great. I see here lifetimes of fascinating possibilities for ingenious young biologists.

BIOLOGICAL TECHNOLOGY

There must be dozens of other areas of study that contain such families of unconventional experiments just waiting to be tried. In biological technology alone there are the experiments required for the selective breeding and herding of sea animals and "farming the oceans", experiments on animal development, in which our new knowledge of embryonic growth would be used in attempts to develop larger brains or stronger muscles; experiments on the closer shaping of animal behavior, not just to make trick animals for the movies, but to make more versatile pets or better dogs for the blind; and experiments on electronic transducers to bring animal sounds into our range of hearing and our sounds into their range of hearing, so as to learn whether dolphins or chimpanzees or Siamese cats might learn to use signals and symbols more as we do if we made it easier for them. This might give us a better understanding of the origins of our own communication and linguistic development over the last few hundred thousand years.

Finally there is an important set of experiments and developments needed for devising more sophisticated machines that would serve biological functions. Not just artificial kidneys, and pacemakers, and artificial hearts, which are all now under study, but things like balancing machines, to help the paralyzed to walk, with motors as compact and powerful and fast as our own muscles, and with feedback circuits as clever as our own balancing. Should these be so hard to devise, for men whose electronic circuits have flown past Mars transmitting pictures? Perhaps not; but the amount of scientific and engineering effort devoted by the nation to such problems is probably less than a ten-thousandth of the space effort.

The balancing problem is part of the interesting problem of making self-guiding automata—artificial cybernetic organisms, or "Cyborgs" as someone has called them—with pattern-perceiving sensory systems, communication systems, and control programs, and with self-contained power sources and motor motions. Such devices will be needed for exploring the hostile surface of the moon and Mars and sending back data, but they would also be useful for exploring sea bottoms and volcanoes and for fire-fighting and other dangerous operations. We are on the edge of understanding how to make such automata, but the problem is still being studied at only a half-dozen centers, and still does not enlist the hundreds of trained and inventive minds that will be needed to make such devices work cheaply and well.

These things I have been talking about are the science fiction of a few years ago, but they are now on the verge of being technically possible, even though they are still "long shots." Many scientists, of course, would be embarrassed to admit that they are professionally interested in such things, and many others might insinuate that if they were not embarrassed they should be. Experiments like these, that touch on our fundamental assumptions about life, encounter a kind of collective unconscious scientific censorship that makes them almost more taboo than the taboos of sex. But, when a few scientists around 1950 broke the taboo on the study of oral contraceptives, the results turned out to be of immense value for the whole human race. Perhaps it is time for some new scientific leaders to break some more taboos in some of these areas and see what further valuable results can be achieved. And perhaps they would find more support today from administrators and granting agencies than they would have found even a few years ago.

It is time for more scientific diversity. The question to be asked is no longer, what does physics have the apparatus and the equations for? It is, rather, what are the curious things in the world? And what are the needs of man?

PATTERNS OF LIVING

Science is not the only area of life where we pursue some lines excessively while neglecting others. It happens throughout our economic and social and political life as well. Just to give one social example here, I think we neglect many important alternatives in our patterns of housing and living. We have automobiles in plenty —and I am no longer one of those who complain about their design; they are remarkably functional and economical and satisfying, and some day they may even be safe! But why should not our magnificent economic and social system be able to give us a similar level of technological skill and competitive cost in the construction of our houses? Or even in our chairs and sofas? These are items that are less than one-hundredth as complex as an automobile but may cost one-fifth as much, even though they are sold in comparable numbers.

And why should the cars have to pass over such ugly streets and highways, which are paid for by the same motorists who choose the cars? To speak of the worst of the eyesores, almost every vista in America is made hideous by the wooden gallows poles and dangling suspender lines of the power companies. A $30,000 home or a $10 million building may have its view defaced from all directions, looking in or looking out, because of a half-dozen $500 power poles whose sole excuse for the intrusion is supposedly commercial or civic economy. I think the daily hideousness of these objects is one of the things that makes us insensitive to other forms of neighborhood blight. Channel some of our dynamic economic energy into removing the poles, and I suspect many lesser uglinesses would be swept away in a wave of neighborhood beautification.

And why should we not be able to have more diversity and

choice in our patterns of houses and lots? Again, there is a coupling of money to conventional patterns of tradition and taboo. If we were to put our houses at the edge of the streets, facing inward on the block, the houses could all look onto a sizable little park in the middle of the block, with trees and a fountain and swings and a place for oldsters to sit and for children to play safely away from the street. Given the pleasure of facing your very own park, who would prefer all these separate private lots with their wasteful driveways and unused areas? Very few, perhaps; but most of us will never know, because our system is focused on a different image and is not flexible enough to give us the option.

In fact, I think there are many different family and neighborhood patterns that we should explore. Try asking people who have traveled and lived in many different types of communities where in their lives they have enjoyed life the most. Surprisingly often the answer is in some form of group living. Many Englishmen say it was in their student days at Oxford. For others it may have been a hitch in the Navy on a good ship. Physicists and chemists still reminisce about the wartime colony at Los Alamos; they learned to share life there because they could not talk about their work. For many University of Chicago graduates, it was the old Howarth House cooperative, with its intellectual explorations and its taste of freedom. Many a Chicago faculty family still looks back with nostalgia to the years in the "pre-fabs" on Fifty-eighth Street or on Sixtieth Street after the war.

Listening to these shared recollections, one begins to wonder whether our conventional pattern of life today, with its separate households and separated age groups, is really giving us the full satisfactions of living. The "pre-fabs" were clusters of two-story buildings around a central court, and they were shabby and crowded and noisy. But in the court, a dozen small children could play safely. Older children could walk to kindergarten and the Lab Schools. The men and many of the women worked or studied within a few blocks and spent little time commuting. And though there was solitude and anonymity for those who wished it, the currents of the world passed through, and there was always conversation, with couples dropping in for spaghetti and wine, or going to political meetings or to plays and movies.

Are we not basically tribal creatures? Good living is with a tribe. At the Marine Biological Laboratories at Woods Hole, Massachusetts, where I have spent several summers, the boundaries between the generations seem to disappear, as well as the boundaries between work and play and between indoors and outdoors and between man and environment. Children and students and teachers walk barefoot in and out of the laboratories, arguing science and studying the odd creatures brought up from the sea. All night they watch the fish embryos developing in the dishes, and they go out before dawn together to catch the big striped bass. The 4-year-olds solemnly examine frogs, the 10-year-olds sell their catch of dogfish to the labs, the 15-year-olds listen to the DNA arguments on the beach or play savage tennis with the senior scientists. No wonder they all want to turn into marine biologists!

Why should we not make environments for ourselves where we can have this kind of diversity and human satisfaction and pleasure of living all year around, instead of just in a student community or a wartime colony or a summer laboratory? I think that many universities and laboratories are neglecting one of their greatest potential attractions, in not trying to arrange environments so that living intellectual communities of this sort could spring up around them. Make a good faculty center for easy and informal interactions, with faculty apartments and guest houses and conference rooms and lounges and terraces and recreation facilities and dining rooms and theaters, and the intellectual dialogue would never stop.

DIVERSITY IN POLITICS

We need more diverse types of communities, and more diverse types of schools—a subject we will come back to in a moment—and more diversity in politics and government. It is not generally realized that half the members of the United States Congress are lawyers, even though lawyers are no more than one-half of 1 per cent of the general population. Such an overrepresentation would have horrified the makers of the Constitution, who anticipated that Congress would consist largely of landowners and leading merchants and professional men like themselves. I think it is easy to see that the present situation has come about, not because we prefer lawyers as our representatives, but because they are the only group with a strong economic incentive for going into politics in great numbers. A lawyer, unlike an engineer or merchant or any other type of candidate, adds to his professional knowledge by being a candidate, and his partners handle his cases for him while he is in office, and he brings them business and comes back afterward with enhanced professional value and useful professional information. It is no surprise that lawyers run for office!

But without wishing to belittle the many good lawyers who are our elected representatives, I think this collective overconcentration of one professional group in our legislatures, even a group that is expert in the laws, is undesirable. Lawyers tend to come from a relatively narrow economic group and their training is also rather narrow, being weak, for example, in the modern psychology and biology that they ought to have, and in the science and technology that are changing the world. It may be their training that is partly responsible for much of our congressional pettifoggery and oratory and black-and-white opinions, and for a tendency to emphasize legalisms and punishment rather than constructive development. The very different approach of the handful of teachers in Congress is especially marked. Diversity, I say! Let us find a way to reduce the financial sacrifices involved in running for office, so that we can have a Congress not only of lawyers but of teachers, scientists, doctors, engineers, businessmen, farmers, ministers, social workers, labor leaders, managers of co-operatives, and housewives. Let us have a body that can speak more accurately for the full range of interests and groups that make up America.

DIVERSITY IN EDUCATION

The area where there is perhaps the greatest need of all for more diversity today is the area of education. Students nowadays can hardly realize how much the alternatives available to them have been closed up by the zealous professionalism of the professors in the last 30 years. In the 1930's, the colleges knew they had been liberalized by John Dewey and they offered what is now sneered at as a "cafeteria system" of education. Yet what an enriched program it permitted us! When I was an undergraduate physics major at Northwestern University I not only took physics and math courses but I had time for electives that included 2 years of French and 3 years of German (Goethe and Schiller), plus astronomy, economics, philosophy, public speaking, music, and a seminar on the origins of war.

Our present survey courses are more thorough and systematic but not so well tailored to each individual's curiosity and enthusiasm. Many colleges have pushed electives almost out of the curriculum, in favor of so-called "honors programs." All too often these should be called "narrows programs," for what they make is one-dimensional men.

It particularly worries me that physics and chemistry majors and other science majors have now lost most of their free electives. Scientists are now rising to executive positions in business and industry and are becoming advisors on major international and military matters. About one-third of all physicists eventually become administrators. I do not want—and I do not think any sane person wants—a world in which the major decisions on technological and military and international affairs are made by one-dimensional men, men who have never had time to explore art or music or history or philosophy or literature or the nontechnical achievements of mankind!

Many of the once-great liberal arts colleges are narrowing their honors programs just like everybody else. How else do you think they get all those graduate fellowships? The ironic thing is that the graduate schools say that this kind of speed-up only gives these students an edge for about six months; and that by the end of the first year the other men who have not had this undergraduate graduate stuff may be doing just as well. The rat race is useless, even in its own terms—except for getting those golden pelletships at the end of the first box.

The only thing that saves us is the fact that the good students learn many things outside the curriculum. I think that in many cases the reputation of the hard-driving schools, both the high schools and the colleges, is not due to the courses or the staff at all, but is due to the quality of the students they are able to get. If you have hot-shots, it makes little difference what you teach them—or whether you teach them at all; they will find out from each other (as the whole human race did!) how to be great contributors to society. The importance of this initial student selection factor has never been sorted out in assessing our schools. Many a school has good graduates not because its education is good but because its students were good when they came in and have not been much damaged.

Even so, the hot-shot dimension is not the only one to be emphasized. Why should we assume or insist that our students have only one important coordinate of variation? This is the fallacy of exams and I.Q. tests. Yes, I want those fast-growing pines, but I also want rosebushes in my classes, and persevering oaks, as I said earlier. It is good that Jacob Getzels and Philip Jackson and others have emphasized recently that there is a dimension of "creativity" in students that has little relation to I.Q. How many other such dimensions of achievement are still to be explored?

We do not even allow for the physiological variations in students. Students, like professors, are not all wakeful or sleepy at the same time. We often start by trying to teach them things when they

—and we—are half-asleep; and then we try to get them to go to sleep when they are wide awake. Many a child's dislike of school may simply reflect his parents' dislike of those awful hours and the half-awake bickering breakfasts before he gets off in the morning.

Would it be impossible to have classes at one time of day for the skylarks and at another time for nightingales? Even professors might like it. Some of the world's greatest leaders napped in the daytime and worked around the clock. Classes in the evening might lead to the best discussions of all if you could sleep in the morning. I have never understood why these possibilities are not seriously examined by educators, who are supposed to know something about the psychology and physiology of learning.

While we are speaking of the right to physiological diversity, let us not forget the right of some of the students to be women. It is easy to show that prejudices and handicaps to women's education still abound. Fathers send sons to college rather than daughters; and not only fathers but deans will cut off a college girl's financial support if she gets married, where they would not cut off a boy's. I have known professors in several departments who refused to take girls as graduate students on the grounds that they would probably get married and not use the education. The "nepotism rules" of many schools result in failure to hire good women teachers if they have the misfortune to be married to good men teachers; so the image of the woman intellectual that the student sees is almost always that of a woman who has renounced marriage. One great university lost a great woman scientist in this way, through refusing to pay her a salary separate from her husband's—until she became famous.

What is worse, however, is the fact that the colleges and counselors do nothing to combat the double standard of the college men, who may learn far-out things in biology or anthropology but are never shaken out of their conventional station-wagon images of what marriage should be. They go on assuming that the college wife, or the graduate-student wife, is the one who shops and cooks and cleans, even if she is carrying courses and trying to do equal work. The delights of student equality extend to men rooming together or to women rooming together, but not to a man and wife in the same apartment. The result of this conventional image—which the girls have often picked up as well as the men—is that American women are concentrating on conventional and subordinate jobs and that, compared to women of other countries, they are making fewer and fewer contributions to our national life, either as educators or editors or scientists or doctors or lawyers or judges or legislators or political leaders. There are fewer women in the United States Congress today than there were thirty years ago. We are only getting half-power out of our educated and intellectual women, and it impoverishes us all.

POVERTY, AUSTERITY, AND OVERWORK

To come back to the narrowing pressures on student life in general, the intellectual and the economic pressures on students today may be neither good education nor good economics. In spite of strikes and disruptions, students may be the most overworked and underpaid class in our society. Their training has now been shown by many studies to be the most important element in the economic development and prosperity of a country, and yet they are not paid as well as their brothers who became plumbers' apprentices. The 18-year-old brother or sister who works in a factory or a store gets off at 5 o'clock and has enough income to have an apartment and a car and books and records and recreation and a paid vacation. He can have guests in and can come in or go out at any hour. But until recently the student has been treated, not like his brothers or parents or teachers, but like a monk with a vow of poverty, austerity, and overwork—a vow which is not even his own vow but has been taken for him. He often works until midnight or later at subjects his brothers might never master, and he is supposed to get money from his family, or borrow it, or be grateful for a fellowship that still leaves him below the poverty level. He frequently has been locked in at night and forbidden to have a car or an apartment, and has little money for his own books or for good meals or concerts. He is given cafeteria fare in cinder-block buildings and never learns to live like a human being. It is an affluent-society parody of medieval monasticism, with the universities—the primary sources of new economic development today—treated as priestly beggars, and with the professors themselves, who have grown up in the system, approving this treatment of the students and feeling, always, that they have too much money and do not work hard enough.

It is an odd 4-year gap in our economic scheme. Students are overworked and underpaid undoubtedly because they are the only group in our society who are too old for child labor laws to protect them and too young to have the support of a union or of professional-market competition—as their parents and their professors have—to help them get more civilized hours and treatment.

And, oh, how long are those hours that we have forced on ambitious students in good schools! No wonder they strike! You professors who have measured the rates of learning, have you measured the optimum number of hours for intellectual work? Do they agree with the standard homework assignment? It is estimated that a medical student is expected to learn 30,000 items of information in his first year, or 100 items per day, if he obeys every demand of the instructors. Is it actually possible to learn at this rate, or does this not simply overload the brain and block any real organization of the material? No wonder the dropout and failure rates are high. No wonder the suicide rate is high.

Men do not become wise and full by studying 14 hours a day, or 10 hours a day, or possibly even 8 hours a day. This is not education for the good life or the good society. There is a limit to human capacity to pack in new knowledge just as there is a limit to the capacity of a stuffed goose. The limit may be no more than a few hours before we need a change of pace for the rest of the day—a period of exercise or recreation or idleness, eating and chatting—if we are really going to assimilate new information and fit it together.

THE NARROW FACULTIES

The trouble is that the faculty itself still thinks this is the only way of education. The student is not taught how to be broad and human because the faculty frequently does not know how to be broad and human. *Nemo dat quod non habet.* No one can give what he does not have. The student is overloaded with information because the professor is overloaded with information, with a piled-up desk and a bulging briefcase. He does not know how to handle it himself, so he passes it on. And many a professor equates education with judgments and grades. I have heard of one man, a kind man in his personal life, who gave out seven F's in a class of 25 undergraduate majors because some students either were not prepared for his 3-hour course or were unwilling to spend 20 hours a week on it, and because he had not the perception or the humanity to tell them earlier that they should not be in the course. This little piece of righteousness will cost these unfortunates hundreds of thousands of dollars in lost fellowships and graduate education and potential job opportunities over their lifetimes. In any other line of work, a man who did such a thing could be sued. In a university, he tells his colleagues it shows how poor the students are today, and they cluck sympathetically. Sometimes such men mellow as they mature, but all too often these black-and-white academics only get more and more self-righteous all the way to retirement.

The student comes for teaching and what he gets is grades. We are hypnotized by grades. They seem so exact and discussable. I have seen departments where one-quarter of the teachers' time and energy was spent in making up exams and grading them. If any administration doubts this, let it measure the ratio. This amount of time spent with individual students could have pulled many of them over the borderline; but we prefer to retreat to written questions. It gives us renewed proof that our students are one-dimensional. What Montessori said should be written on every bluebook in letters of fire: "The business of a teacher is to teach, not to judge." The business of a professor is to give, not grades, but intellectual contagion.

Do not misunderstand my criticisms here. I think the academic life can be the most varied and imaginative and interesting life in the world, and I love it. But I am talking about its distortions and about how they narrow it from what it might become. Its great men are so very great and its little men are so little. And it pains me when I see one of those academic men who has deliberately narrowed himself to an intellectual pinpoint and has cut off all that life might be. Emerson must have been thinking of such men when he said: "The state of society is one in which the members have suffered amputation from the trunk, and strut about so many walking monsters—a good finger, a neck, a stomach, an elbow, but never a man."

The academic world is perhaps no worse in this respect than the world of government or the world of business, but it is sad all the same. The teacher is the one man who most needs to know what it is to be a complete man with wholeness and diversity and humor. When his vision is distorted, the vision of a whole generation may be warped.

I think it is time to say loudly and clearly that the interval of higher education should be an interval of learning to live like cultured human beings instead of like monks and academics. Instead of overload and punishment let us have more creative leadership. Along with excellence let us enjoy diversity. Let us try to find ways in which students can be given the money and leisure they ought to have as valuable apprentices in an affluent society. Let us bring up a generation of young adults full of the delight of living, interested in many things, and knowing not only how to be intellectual and concerned but how to be full and creative men.

I think that this goal I have suggested, of trying to make the college years more humane, more cultured, and more diverse, is just a part of a new educational revolution that will totally change the structure of our schools in the next 20 years. This revolution may be even more thoroughgoing than the revolution that was made by John Dewey and the other reformers 70 years ago, when they swept out the obsolete and stuffy classical education of the 19th century and redefined the goals of education as education for society and education for living.

Today our education has indeed become an excellent education for our society, so far as its professional content is concerned, but it is still obsolete and clumsy in its teaching methods. Since World War II, a revolution has occurred in information and communication and in our knowledge of the biology and psychology of the brain and the psychology of learning. It is beginning to be urgent for us to adapt our educational system to take account of these advances. Mass education up until now has been hard and punitive, with more of the stick than of the carrot. It has been hardest and most punitive in the colleges, where many departments and schools are actually proud to have standards so strict that they flunk one-third of their freshmen.

But it is now possible to move away from this traditional pattern. It has become clear that the psychology of positive reinforcement, of encouraged curiosity and reward, works much better than the psychology of negative reinforcement, as great teachers have always known. As the psychologist Lawrence Kubie says, "Efficient learning is never hard." We do not teach football by giving exams, but by contagion, and the students learn it and play it spontaneously. Why should we teach Chaucer differently? Students and faculty did not crowd the halls to hear Agassiz lecture, or A. J. Carlson or Fermi, just because they were going to get an exam on it later. If a school is so unlucky that it does not have a teacher of Chaucer or of Western civilization or of physics who can teach by contagion, the students will demand leave to go to some other subject where we do have such a man. The enthusiasm of learning and of discovering for oneself is more important to the university and to the student and to his final performance in society than any particular coverage of subject matter.

The new psychology has brought us new discoveries and new methods. At the University of Chicago, Benjamin Bloom and others have emphasized the effect of early enrichment, and of preschool tutoring at ages one to four, on later I.Q. and school success. We now have programmed electric typewriters to teach reading and writing to children of two to four as well as to retarded readers, and the new ITA phonetic alphabet is speeding up early reading in its own way. At higher grades, the discovery of the power of rapid-reinforcement methods offers new ease and success. Programmed learning and teaching machines and "Tutortexts" offer the student individual instruction in which he can go at his own pace, and they promise to make spelling and geography and physics and anatomy and other subjects both easier and more quickly mastered.

The new ideas have already made a revolution across the nation in the teaching of high-school science courses, and efforts are well under way to create science programs with the same exciting immediacy all the way down to the kindergarten level. In fact it now appears that the whole difficulty with many subjects is that we have been teaching them too late. A 7-year-old can learn reading and writing more easily than an 18-year-old can, and we are now finding that he may also learn about sets and binary arithmetic and rates-of-change and the difference between mass and weight more easily than many college sophomores.

The difficulty today is that these remarkable new methods have not yet been drawn together into a unified educational approach. We have a better engine, a better transmission, and a better steering mechanism, but they have not yet been fitted together to make a complete car. It seems very likely that, when they are all put together, these new developments in education will reinforce each other and will make possible further gains that would not come from any one alone. Pre-school reading and writing would make room for beginning science in the early grades. Binary arithmetic in the second grade may make a child ready and eager for number theory and computer programming in the sixth. Rates-of-change at age 7 would permit introduction to economics at 13.

What is needed now, for several reasons, is to get out of our standard educational structure and to set up complete new kinds of pilot schools to try out this new personal and concrete and manipulative education in an integrated program all the way from age 1 to 21 and beyond. We need to try schools of several different kinds, in different types of communities, in slum areas and rich suburbs, in company towns and scientific laboratory communities, to find out which kind of program under different circumstances produces the most alert and creative citizens. If we can find some educational leaders who will take the initiative in establishing private schools of this sort, or who can persuade some forward-looking school boards to try them out, this may be the educational adventure of the next decade most satisfying to impatient students.

I think that, if we put together all the speed-ups and simplifications that these new methods make possible, the children in such schools would no longer be overworked. The subjects we now teach them might be mastered in a much shorter school day, perhaps no more than 3 or 4 hours. There would be less boredom and resistance in school and more time for creative leisure outside. Some parents may shudder at this, because they do not want the children home half the day. But with the new trends of productivity and automation in our adult life, perhaps creative leisure is one of the things we need to teach children earliest. And if we let the adult's leisure enrich the children's leisure, homework might even become home play. The interaction between the generations might make for better relations than we have had for years. In fact the children, with their shorter hours, going home from school may soon meet the adults, with their new leisure, going back, hoping to learn in a more voluntary and serious way the subjects they missed in all their years of report-card education.

All this would change our stereotyped pattern of education in a remarkable way. The intense program of work now imposed across a few years in the late teens—where we have to study all day and all night because the earlier grades have taught us so little— might be replaced by an easier longitudinal pattern that would start with easy and fast learning methods at age 1 or 2 and would then go on all our lives for 2 or 3 or 4 hours a day. The children and the college students and the leisured adults might acquire a new attitude toward education. Formal teaching might blend inseparably into more individual and creative leisure-time activities, such as building boats together or learning music or ballet or skiing —or studying embryos and catching striped bass before dawn. Education would be by contagion and long discussion, and the generations might learn to talk to each other again.

A lifetime ago we made the transformation to education for living. It is time now to make the transformation to education for wholeness, for delight, and for diversity.

II

The Two Faces of Perception

*A model of man's decision-networks helps us understand our subjec-
tive-objective oneness with the world.*

THE NATURE of perception has always been one of the hardest
things in the world to explain. We are too close to it to be able to
see it clearly. The problem is somewhat like the problem of the fish
who went up to the fish-scientist and asked him to explain the sea.
The fish said, "What is this sea you scientists talk about? You say
you are practical and you believe in objective things, in what can
be seen and touched. Well, if there is such a thing as the sea, if it is
real, point it out to me. Show me where it is." And the fish-scientist
is supposed to have had a hard time answering him.

Actually, of course, a fish must understand quite a lot about
the resistance of water and where the top and bottom are. A two-
year-old child knows quite a lot about the ocean of air around him
which cannot be seen or pointed to, but which pushes on kites and
clouds and which he can blow into a balloon. The problem of perception, however, is far more subtle. The ocean of perception, in
which we live and move and have our being, not only cannot be
pointed to, but its resistance cannot be measured nor its motions
felt. Perception is so simple anyone can do it, yet it is so universal
and so indivisible that the philosophers have written their longest
and most contradictory treatises in trying to explain it.

However, I have begun to suspect that this problem may be
like the old problem of "motion," which the medieval philosophers
also wrote long and involved treatises about. We now realize that
their trouble was that they had the wrong concepts, the wrong language, and no experiments. Once Galileo and Newton had straight-
ened out the concepts of momentum and force and acceleration, any
bright adolescent could learn to calculate the motions of pendulums
and projectiles quite accurately. In the analysis of perception, I

think the new experimental and theoretical work that is now coming out of the biological and psychological laboratories may straighten out our concepts in much the same way, and may likewise open the door to a new era of understanding.

This could be of the greatest importance to us. Perception has two faces, the subjective and the objective. The objective world is easy to talk about. This is the ordinary world of common speech, of things that can be pointed to, for which we have developed a public language, with nouns and verbs that every child understands. It is the subjective world that has been hard to discuss, and even embarrassing. Objective science shrinks from it, as from religion. Its important elements cannot be pointed to; and for its more general and personal elements we often have no publicly agreed-upon terms at all, or only misleading ones, like "heart" and "soul" and "self," derived from ancient theologies and mental theories.

Yet this is the area where primary perception lies, and knowledge and judgment and will. What else is the main concern of our efforts with our children? If we impose on them the terms of a medieval philosophy, they may get as twisted in their lives as if we tried to teach them physics in terms of vortices and phlogiston. I think a better understanding of the true relation of the subjective world to the objective world, both for parents and children, might help us to cure many of our personal and social misdirections. It might help all of us to plunge more deeply and satisfyingly into the real, instead of using up our lives in struggling to reach pseudo-goals that are by their very nature will-o'-the-wisps and unattainable. Perception is the first thing we experience and the last thing we understand. It is the beginning of knowledge and also, in some sense, the end of it. A more accurate understanding of perception might change our individual and social relations as dramatically as a more accurate understanding of motion a few hundred years ago changed our technological achievements.

It will be evident that I come to these problems as a physicist and biophysicist. I worked for many years on the theory of the colors of organic molecules, then more directly on the physics of perception and the optical and electrical aspects of vision, and more recently on how the visual network or any "sensory-motor decision-network" like the brain can organize its information so as to know something about the regularities of the external world. There is a larger body of interest by physical scientists in such questions than most people realize. The physics of perception has not been fashionable in this century, but in earlier times many physicists worked on it, from Kepler to Kant and from Maxwell to Mach. What can a man or an organism know about the world and his relation to it? How can an organism perceive? Or more fundamentally, how can matter think? These are epistemological and philosophical questions, but if we are to find twentieth-century answers for them, modern physical thinking must contribute, as well as modern biology and psychology. The answers may even be important for physics. For, as the quantum theorist David Bohm has emphasized, physics "is basically a mode of extending our perception of the world," and the elementary operations of physics are insecure to us unless we can demonstrate that they are consistent with the elementary operations of perception.

Recently a number of physical scientists have come forward with a personal "operational" approach to perception which fits in particularly well, I think, with our new views of the brain and of neural networks, although it has been misunderstood by most physicists. This approach was foreshadowed by Ernst Mach eighty years ago in his book *The Analysis of Sensations,* which influenced Freud. It has now been developed in several different ways by Percy Bridgman in his final book, *The Way Things Are;* by Erwin Schrödinger in *Mind and Matter* and in the epilogue to *What Is Life?;* by Michael Polanyi in *Personal Knowledge;* and by David Bohm in the appendix on "Physics and Perception" in his book *Relativity.* Support for this new personalism from the biological side has also been given by the biologist George Wald and by the neuroanatomist Roger Sperry in their chapters in *New Views of the Nature of Man.*

What I want to do here is to outline how some of the recent experimental and theoretical work on neural networks and perception can be fitted together with these personal and operational views so as to give a more coherent and operational theory of perception. I want to show how we can go step by step from the objective scientific evidence to its application in interpreting the subjective phenomena of perception, just as we can go from the objective study of eyeballs and cameras to the interpretation of the subjective phenomena of our own eyesight. When this kind of connection is made explicit, it can clear up many of the linguistic difficulties and can be the basis of a more accurate grammar of perception than we have had before. And I believe, as we shall see, that the results can even illuminate many of the great subjective insights of the saints and philosophers, which can now be restated in more objectively derived and less paradoxical language.

OBJECTIVE MODELS OF THE BRAIN

Objective Models as Subjective Mediators

Perception, like any other field, can be approached from various starting points. But I think it is important not to begin, as so many have done, either by trying to imagine the blank mind of a baby, or else by trying to imagine what "primary sensations" we are "really" having right now. These traditional approaches beg the very questions we want to answer. I think we encounter the fewest difficulties if we start simply and objectively from where we are now in relation to each other, that is, from this present conversational reality where we talk together as persons educated in a common culture, speaking or reading our common public language of description and abstraction and persuasion, about things that can be pointed to and described in common objective terms.

If we do this, it is then a fairly easy and convincing jump to the interpretation of at least some of our subjective experience. To demonstrate this, take the case of eyeballs and eyesight. We all believe, of course, that we do have eyeballs like those of other men, eyeballs through which we see the objective world, and which are the "mediators," so to speak, of our subjective visual experiences. But have you ever asked yourself the question, "How do I *know* that I have eyes—or a head or a brain—when I cannot see them?" In some ways, it is a childish question, so simple that the proofs are familiar and are confirmed daily and hourly. Yet it is important as well as entertaining to spend a little time to see how the proofs go, because the eyeball example is the prototype, I believe, of the way in which other types of objective evidence (like that on neural networks) can be used in interpreting other aspects of subjective experience.

Our proofs for the existence of our own eyeballs are of three types. First, from witnesses; second, from physical analogy; and third, from our own senses, including touch and the visual evidence of shadows and mirrors. Thus, for witnesses, I can take unsophisticated children one at a time, and test their veracity on other objects. "Billy, does the dog have eyes?" "Yes." And he points to them. He should know!—for I pointed them out to him just last week, saying "Those are the dog's eyes." (We are a consistent language community.)

"And do I have eyes?" "Yes." And he points again, in a certain unique direction. And I can make the same test with Tommy and Jack, and they all say the same. And I know that they are eager in checking each other, and that they are reliable in pointing out dogs, which I can see; and airplanes behind my head, which I can turn and see. So it seems reasonable to believe that they are talking about something objective when they talk about and point in this funny direction to my "eyes," which—as they will be sure to tell me!—I can *not* turn and see for myself.

The second argument is from physical analogy, where I note that I interact with light bulbs and with sunlight in much the same way that I see another person's eyes interact. A card or a piece of glass interrupts or distorts the light for Billy and for the camera, and for me; so I can believe that the principles of optics, and of image-forming lenses like theirs, determine at least some aspects of my subjective experience.

The third and strongest line of evidence for my eyes comes from my own senses. I touch my hair, face, nose, eyelids, lashes, eyeballs, and find them all like Billy's. I can see my nose from two unique perspectives, and see my finger touching it, and I can see my own lids and lashes, even if they are rather blurred. And on the wall or floor I can see shadows of my head, hair, nose, and eyesockets, and of one eyelid closing as I close it.

The mirror evidence provides especially strong confirmation and detail. I look in the mirror and I see Billy's body and clothes and eyes repeated there, and Billy's every movement is copied simultaneously by this mirror-Billy. But then beside him in the mirror, I see that other body, wearing *my* clothes, and copying *my* finger-movements as I touch my nose, and copying *my* eyelid-blink, though it has a head and hair and eyes that I have never seen directly. And I know the laws of the mirror and I can infer that I do have eyes, as Billy does, even when the mirror is not there.

The sharing of language is the first proof that men are equivalent, but whenever I think about the conclusiveness of the detailed evidence from mirrors, I wonder whether the mirror may not have changed the self-understanding of men more than any other invention after language. In the mirror, even a tyrant realizes himself to be another man, and naked. It must have exerted throughout history a steady pressure for humility and democracy.

Knowledge of Brains

I have gone into these types of proof because I think they can be extended to our central question here, which is how our brains work and whether this can throw any light on our subjective aspects of perception. We cannot see our own brains in a mirror or examine their internal workings—although a psychologist or neurosurgeon, if he had to cut into our heads, might tell us something about our electrical potentials or structural abnormalities. But we can examine in considerable detail how the brains of animals work and how those of other people work, and this may give us a good deal of analogical understanding. Most of what I have to say here is based on this kind of detailed objective examination of brain models and theories.

It is true that our knowledge of the brain is very incomplete. Probably it always will be, because the human brain, with its vast number of something like 10^{11} nerve cells or neurons—a hundred billion or so—and with its interconnections or synapses between these neurons perhaps a thousand times more numerous still, is the most complicated thing that man has ever tried to study. Man's genetic apparatus in his chromosomes, which determines the growth and interrelation of all the structures in his body, is among the most complex in the animal world. But his individual brain is far more complex even than that, because it somehow enfolds in addition all of the specific richness of his individual experience and all that he knows or dreams or creates of science and religion and literature and human relations. I think that the brain may go on being studied long after physics and chemistry and all the rest of biology have become as clear as Euclid's geometry.

Nevertheless, I think our partial new understanding of the brain today, though still rudimentary, may have finally put us on the right track in understanding perception. Many of the recent experiments on the brain show a new and close relation to some of our subjective experience. And even where this evidence is still incomplete, it can be explained and pieced out with some new theoretical models which bridge the gap and which are very illuminating indeed.

It may be helpful to describe the theoretical models first. Good theoretical models are not to be despised. They often play a crucial role in simplifying a complex problem. Galileo's idealization of the "free body" and Newton's "point particle" were what first made physics tractable. For the brain, one of the influential early models was Descartes's automaton obeying physical and chemical principles, with nerve channels carrying inputs to the center for decision.

In the last few years, the most fruitful theoretical models of man and man's brain have been those derived from feedback and communications theory and systems theory. Norbert Wiener proposed a model of the organism as a cybernetic or goal-directed system. He said that in trying to lift a glass or catch a rabbit, a man or an animal gets back sensory inputs or feedbacks that measure the distance from the goal, and that these sensory signals are then amplified by the muscles so as to close the gap. There are different goals at different times, but each response is like that of the stabilizing or goal-seeking response of an electrical feedback circuit, or of a target-seeking guided missile.

Some of the higher operations of the brain have also been modeled by computer systems. The most sophisticated attempts of this sort would include the pattern-perceiving machine or Perceptron of Frank Rosenblatt, and the theorem-proving and general problem-solving machines of Allen Newell and Herbert Simon, which can search for theorems in geometry or can teach themselves in successive trials to play a better game of chess. Today these mechanical-electronic systems still operate on a "single channel" of inputs, or on only a few channels; but some day we may begin to make more complex systems, with "parallel processing" of thousands or millions of multiple input channels, and when we do, I believe their capacity for distinguishing patterns and producing alternative responses may become astonishing.

In addition to these models with real "hardware," there are also today some more generalized theoretical models of "general systems" and of "concrete living systems," as discussed by James G. Miller and others. These are attempts to examine in a general way the relations among the subsystem components that every living system must have to survive—such as information channels, memory, decision centers, motor outputs, and reproductive elements—and to study the relation of the subsystems and the system itself to the "supersystem" or environment, in what Simon has called the "architecture of complexity."

The Brain as a Sensory-Motor Decision-System

But the model that I think is particularly illuminating for the perception problem combines several of these features in a "sensory-motor decision-system." This is the kind of model that is diagrammed in Figure 1. On the left side the three small circles represent the thousands or millions of sensory receptor cells, like the rods and cones of the eye or the auditory hair cells of the ear. The successive heavy arrows moving downward and away from these receptors in curved arcs represent the neurons and their interconnections in successive stages or echelons of the nervous network. The most direct routes of this sort might be "reflex arcs." They end in

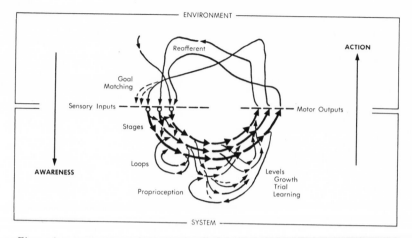

Fig. 1. A sensory-motor decision network interacting with the environment

heavy terminal arrows on the right side of Figure 1, which are supposed to represent the thousands or millions of amplified motor
outputs, making muscular motions, glandular secretions and the
like, which influence the environment or external world. The bottom half of Figure 1 could be thought of as a very schematic diagram of the eye, the brain, and the right hand, as seen from above.

The lighter curving lines from the output region on the right
side of the diagram, curving upward across the top of the figure and
around to the left again, represent the physical motions and other
effects in the external world which are again detected and checked
by their optical and other signals to the sensory cells, which in turn
feed back into the system network for another round of analysis and
outputs.

We will discuss the various features of this diagram in more detail later. But it is clear that two extreme kinds of such sensory-motor decision-systems can be distinguished: non-learning systems and
learning systems. The non-learning system is essentially what is
found in insects. It is a system entirely, or almost entirely, "wired
up" or "preprogrammed" in advance by the creature's genetic instructions during growth and development, so that it can find the
right food and the right kind of mate and build the right nest automatically from the moment it emerges from the cocoon, without the
necessity for the individual organism to learn any new responses
from its experiences. The responses of such creatures can only be
changed phylogenetically, in the species as a whole, by the Dar-
winian mechanism of small individual variations, with natural selection of those more successful in survival and reproduction.

Learning systems, on the other hand, are typical of the higher mammals and human beings. It is obvious that they must be built on a large preprogrammed base, such as our internal autonomic nervous sytem which regulates heartbeat and breathing and digestion, and our sensory-motor reflex arcs, which make us blink or pull back almost uncontrollably from a burn or a blow. But the more complex behavior of human beings is almost entirely learned behavior, which has its own kind of internal natural selection. The system is capable of making variable responses to a given situation and is able to assess these responses and to repeat those which are successful from some point of view, and to stop making those which are unsuccessful. The new learned behavior has to be acquired and shaped within the individual. Undoubtedly this is the major reason for our long childhood, as well as for our adaptability to new environments and for our creativity in situations we have never met before.

Reafferent Stimulation

One of the important features of this model is that it is able to fit in a considerable body of recent experimental evidence about the mechanisms that humans and animals use for perceiving and validating and adjusting to the external world.

For example, it has now been found experimentally by Robert Ditchburn and his co-workers and by Lorrin Riggs and his co-workers that constant motion of the eyeballs is necessary for visual perception. The motions are too tiny and fast to be seen by the unaided eye. Their amplitudes are less than one minute of arc and their frequencies are in the range from 50 to 150 cycles per second. Nevertheless, if they are compensated by optical or electronic devices so that the image is exactly stabilized on the retina, vision disappears within a fraction of a second. Presumably the motions produce varying inputs which prevent the retinal cells from becoming fatigued, or adapted. This explains, incidentally, why we cannot see the blood vessels of our own eyes, although they lie in front of the retina; their shadows stay fixed in the same place, so that the sensory cells become adapted to them and they do not appear in vision. "Vision is an a.c. phenomenon and not a d.c. phenomenon," as Ditchburn has said.

But this is a particular and very simple case of the more general "reafferent stimulation" that Richard Held and his co-workers have now shown to be absolutely necessary for early visual learning in animals and for adaptation to visual distortion in human subjects. Reafferent stimulation is the kind of visual or other stimulation, or set of new input signals, that comes from the environment as the result of the system's own motor outputs, as indicated in the environmental arcs at the top of Figure 1. (This differs from the "proprioceptive" signals which come back internally from the muscles and indicate their state of activity. These are symbolized by one of the light lower arrows traveling from right to left across the bottom of the diagram in Figure 1.)

Held's experiment of the "passive and active kittens" is a particularly convincing demonstration of the need for reafferent stimulation in learning. In this experiment, two kittens are kept in the dark after birth, except for a few minutes each day when they are placed in an apparatus where one kitten pulls the other around. They both have the same variation of visual patterns when they are in this apparatus; but for the active kitten, these variations are the result of the kitten's own muscular movements, while for the passive kitten they are unrelated to the muscle movements. After a few of these experiences in the apparatus, if the kittens are tested near the edge of a table or "visual cliff," it is found that the active kitten braces himself or draws back from the edge; while the kitten whose visual experiences have been passive acts as though it could not see or interpret the edge, and may fall over.

Held's experiments on human visual adaptation confirm these results. Students are asked to put on distorting glasses that tilt or rotate the visual field. It is found that they can adapt or correct rather rapidly for the distortion if they are allowed to move themselves about for a few minutes, or perhaps to wheel themselves about the campus in a wheelchair with the glasses on. But if they are only passively moved or wheeled about, they do not adapt.

These various experiments seem to prove that the images or signals that come into the brain from the external world are required not to be either stationary or randomly moving, or they will be either invisible or uninterpretable. They can be seen and organized and corrected only if some essential additional information or regularities have been provided by the relation between the changes of these signals and the system's own motor manipulations.

Functional Geometry

I think a reafferent-stimulation mechanism of this kind can also help us to explain an old puzzle. This is the puzzle of how the somewhat random cells of the individual retina, differently arranged from one individual to the next, can arrive at a common and highly precise geometry of the external world. How can we see straight lines, or parallel lines? And how can we agree on their straightness and other regularities so exactly?

Part of the answer, of course, is that the eye has certain built-in pattern-perception and invariance-detecting mechanisms. This was demonstrated by recent work on frog vision by Jerry Lettvin and his co-workers, and it has been confirmed by the discovery of the "edge-detectors" in the visual cortex of the cat by David Hubel and Torsten Wiesel, and by the discovery of velocity-detecting cells in the retina itself by Horace Barlow and co-workers.

But I think that these pattern-organizing elements, although they form a base for the structuring of higher processes, are still on too small a scale and too individually variable to answer a large geometrical question such as, How can we see straight lines?

Certainly, it seems difficult to believe that a *static* map on the retina could be interpreted by you and by me to indicate the same object pattern, such as straightness, because the image will fall on one set of cells in your eye and a different set of cells, differently arranged, in my eye.

But if we use reafferent stimulation—that is, a *dynamic* mechanism in which we move the images back and forth on the retina—the problem suddenly becomes much more simple. For example, a way in which we can tell whether the top edge of a blackboard is straight is to look at the left side of the edge and then to look at the right side. If the image of the left side falls on a certain set of cells in your eye, and if it continues to fall on the same set of cells as you move your eye across to the right side, then the line is straight. For no S-curve or general irregular curve can continue to fall on the same array of cells in your eye as you move it.

In short, I am suggesting that the simplest way to organize the geometrical space of the external world is by looking for *invariances under displacement*. I call this the principle of "functional geometry," meaning a dynamic approach to geometry rather than a static approach in terms of mapping. The operation of "invariance under displacement" can be used by any eye and retina to single out as unique such important geometrical pattern elements and regularities as straight lines, parallel lines, and equidistant lines, as well as things like uniform circular arcs (provided the eyeball can rotate about the optic axis, as indeed it can).

It is interesting to see that this method of extracting pattern regularities is very similar to the methods used for generating mathematically perfect surfaces, such as spherical and plane surfaces, in high-precision optical work. John Strong, the designer of high-precision ruling engines, has described in detail the methods of grinding and lapping for generating perfect spheres, perfect planes, perfect helixes, perfect equidistant spacings of a ruled grating, and perfect gears with high-precision angular spacings of the gear teeth. Basically, his methods do not involve measurements, but simply involve sliding and lapping one surface, such as a spherical surface, over another which just fits it.

In this kind of displacement-invariance method, you do not use any rulers, and you do not have any centers! The spheres define their own centers and radii as they are polished, and the numerical values are not even measured. If you try to specify the center, it turns out that you damage the approach to sphericity because you are "over-determining" the system. It has to determine itself. In commenting on this elimination of measurement and external centers, Strong says, "the methods of highest precision are all primitive methods."

Does it not seem likely that a biological system would need to use some primitive general high-precision method of this sort? For the eye has no x-axes and y-axes for Cartesian-coordinate determination of the patterns of figures. It has no method, as far as I know, for determining the "shortest distance between two points."

In fact, the elimination of these classical bases of measurement and construction means that functional geometry gives us a new axiomatic basis for geometry. We suddenly realize that Euclidean geometry is "string geometry;" it is the kind of geometry you get by drawing on the sand using a piece of string. This can be seen in the definitions: a straight line is the "shortest distance between two points"—of the kind that is represented by a stretched string. A circle is the "locus of points equidistant from a given point"—using a length of string as a measure of distance.

Cartesian geometry, on the other hand, is "box geometry." It is the geometry of a European house, in which the walls are made of bricks that step up 1, 2, 3, 4, 5 . . . units. The floor is made of tiles that march out 1, 2, 3, 4, 5 . . . units, north and east. (I suspect that the Greeks, with the bowed-out columns and arched floors of their temples, could never have invented Cartesian geometry.) But now we come to functional geometry, which differs from these static, locus-of-a-point, geometries, and which has no axes, no centers, or "origin," no measures of distance, no guarantee that some primordial axes are at right angles to each other—and which gets along extremely well without all this initial apparatus.

Incidentally, this even throws a new light on the "parallel postulate." In functional geometry, the parallel postulate is immediately provable, because if two lines are invariant under displacement along them—that is, if parallelism is defined by that kind of invariance—then if they do not meet in one region, they will never meet, because they are invariant. Therefore two parallel lines so defined will never meet. What I suspect is that Euclid or his predecessors had a kind of intuitive biological sense of this sort. Perhaps Euclid felt that two parallel lines ought never to meet, and since this cannot be proved by any method such as the "interior-angle" construction from the other axioms, he felt it had to be added as an additional axiom.

The kind of discriminations that can be made by functional geometry also raise an interesting question. The distinction between a "straight-line" displacement (x- and y-axes of the eyeball) without rotation (about the z-axis), and a "slightly-curved line" displacement with a little bit of rotation (about the z-axis) does not depend on functional geometry, since both patterns may be equally invariant under the right muscle-motions. Rather, it depends on the accuracy of the "analog system" monitoring muscle movements, which tells one how much the muscles (of the z-axis) are moving. We thus have a lower-accuracy analog system for detecting some features of the pattern and a high-accuracy invariant array system for detecting other features of the pattern. This is like the boy polishing a spherical mirror, who cannot control the curvature very accurately even though he gets a very accurate spherical surface in every case. We cannot in fact tell the difference between a straight line and a slightly curved one unless we have another line nearby to compare it to (which converts the judgment from an analog judgment to an invariance-judgment). The analog and the invariance mechanisms are then two mechanisms working on top of each other. The activities of the muscles of the eye (analog) do not in themselves define a very accurate axis system for the movement of the eye, and when one is in a darkened room the image seems to drift around in quite an arbitrary way. But when one looks at a circle or an object with geometrical regularities, the object itself, by its invariances, can determine its own centers and axes with high precision.

The simple and powerful thing about functional geometry is that it can generate its basic elements by the simplest possible dynamic test: invariance under displacement. What could be simpler for the muscles than a very roughly directed displacement? What requirement could be simpler for a network than that it merely be able to indicate when a pattern is the same as one before? Is not this simple method, so similar in its operations to the methods used in the highest-precision machine work and optical work, the kind of method a biological system would be likely to evolve, which would give it maximum precision with minimum requirements?

The Search for Invariances

It seems possible that the dynamic search for invariances may even be a general principle of organization in the higher-order processes in the brain. Dynamic invariance means that motor activity leads to feedback through the external world into the sensory inputs again, as indicated by the curved arrows traveling from right to left at the top of Figure 1. If the sensory inputs are not the same as they were before, there can be some goal-seeking or goal-matching activity until the invariance is established—until, for example, the eye is being moved along the straight line by the muscles again. But this will then be a self-maintaining loop, with repeated stimulation and interconnections along the same channels, that is, with maximum "reinforcement" built up for *this* kind of muscular response to *this* kind of stimulus pattern.

Recently, the physicists Peter Putnam and Robert Fuller have conjectured that self-reinforcing and self-maintaining loops of this sort may also be characteristic of the internal network structure, somewhat like the earlier "ringing" loops postulated by the psychologist D. O. Hebb. Such loops are diagrammed in the bottom half of Figure 1, along with some other higher-level interconnections. Each loop established would represent a new functional regularity "discovered" by the system in the environment or, more exactly, in the system-environment relationship. Once a loop is established, it might be opened and closed—turned off or on—by the chemical or other state of the organism; perhaps closed whenever the system comes back to the initial state or condition under which the loop was first established.

Several authors have reached rather similar formulations of these higher-order problems. The search for invariants has been called "invarianting" by Bohm, to whom I am indebted for a long correspondence on these problems; he compares it to a mathematical "rotation" or "diagonalization" of the "sensory-input matrix." The biophysicist Peter Greene has compared the jumping between states of the system—or between Gestalts, or perhaps self-reinforcing loops—to the jumping between the holistic quantum states of an atomic system. There may also be higher-order families of loops, such as the families of muscle motions generated, say, in scanning familiar or regular patterns. Or conversely, as Putnam and Fuller say, the higher-order loops may provide an alternation or other mechanism for resolving conflict between lower-order loops. This "intersection" of lower-order loops could be the "bisociation" which Arthur Koestler, in his book *The Act of Creation,* has proposed as the basis for the creative act.

Anatomically, any such perceptual growth to higher-order patterns would demand continual neurophysiological growth, with some random variations, among neural interconnections. This is suggested in Figure 1 by the dashed lines near the bottom, which might suggest potential new trial connections ready to form and be tested for their fit into self-stabilizing loops.

We see that the "most interesting" regions of the network, the regions having the most points of conflict and of novelty of interconnection, the regions at the "growing edge" of creativity and change, might be where the highest-order loops of this kind are in process of formation. This would be where the accumulated knowledge of the system is combined with an ever changing search to solve new dilemmas. These regions would form creative centers of control and decision among all the less complex subprocesses that are being used and fitted together. Such creative control centers are perhaps as close as we can come objectively to the location of a central "will" or "soul" in such a decision-system.

Sperry has emphasized that such higher-order centers can properly be spoken of as controlling their lower-order processes, rather than just being controlled by them. He says:

> [Just as] a molecule is in many respects the master of its inner atoms and electrons . . . [so] when it comes to brains, remember that the simpler electric, atomic, molecular, and cellular forces and laws, though still present and operating, have been superseded by the configurational forces of higher-level mechanisms. At the top, in the human brain, these include the powers of perception, reason, judgment and the like, the operational, causal effects and forces of which are equally or more potent in brain dynamics than are the outclassed inner chemical forces. . . . .

It is interesting to note that a decision-system of the type we are describing cannot observe itself very accurately, in spite of its numerous internal sensors and loops of various sorts. The growing edge will always be hard to relate to or to specify in terms of any of its other established knowledge. The system may be able to make useful new interconnections—just as organic evolution does—without knowing how or why or being able to predict or justify them. "Consciousness will always be one dimension above compre-hensibility," as the biochemist Gösta Ehrensvärd has said. If this kind of network is like our brains, then for our creative activity we simply have to trust the "wisdom of the body"—which is in this case the neuroanatomical wisdom of the mind—to lead us to func-tional regularities and understanding and organization of our sys-tem-and-world beyond what we know how to analyze.

Properties of Functional Geometry

Before turning to the main question ahead of us, which is how these objective models and theories of brains might be related to our subjective experience, it is important to spend a little time ex-amining some of the rather unusual and unexpected properties that these models have.

Take functional geometry, for example; or any other dynamic-invariance method of detecting geometrical relationships in the field of view. It is easy to see, first, that such a method is indepen-dent of the location of individual retinal cells, and second, that it is independent of their sensitivity. The method only requires that when the eye is scanned from one invariant region to another, the invariants fall on the same set of cells after scanning, whether the individual cells are left or right, good or bad—or even missing, as in the "blind spot." I think this gives us at last the explanation of why straight lines or other patterns are seen as continuing right across the blind spot. What we "see" are not the raw signals from the image, but their invariances. We do not see objects, but rela-tionships.

But in addition, the method of functional geometry is indepen-dent of distortion of the image on the retina—or on the visual cor-tex of the brain, where the projection is known to be split and twisted. For as the eye scans a straight line, the image of one end of the line may fall on a distorted or crooked curve on the retina; but if the image of the other end of the line after the movement contin-ues to fall on the *same* crooked curve, then the line is invariant—which means straight. It is sometimes forgotten by visual theorists that the brain has no separate microscope to look at the retina, or at the cortex, to see whether the image is geometrically straight; all it can know is what it can determine from functional operations, like invariances, within the network. It is obvious that mechanical twisting or spatial distortion of the network inside, or crookedness of the network patterns in space, make no difference to perception as long as the interconnections are unchanged. (This must be so, simply because of the great anatomical and folding differences found at autopsy between the brains of different persons who could see equally well.)

What is defined by such a functional method of perception, therefore, is not geometrical regularities in the internal world but regularities in the external world. The variations from one person to another—genetic variations in network geometry between parent and child, or developmental variations from the child to the grown man, or variations in the shape of the image, or in the anatomy of the retina or cortex, or in the internal structure of the network—all become irrelevant. This theoretical method thus fits what we know experimentally: that two persons, such as you and I, can both look at a line independently and decide whether it is straight or not, and that we will usually agree within the accuracy of our visual focusing. And this is not just a "nominalist" test connected with the fact that society has called such lines by a special name; it is a uniqueness property of these unusual lines, which I believe would cause us both to single out such lines for special attention even if society had never given them a name before.

Regularities determined by such a method are therefore regularities in an objective and *public space,* in spite of the fact that the representation of them is carried out entirely in a private network. This is an extremely important capability for biological organisms to have. With functional geometry, the brain's representation of the external world can "transcend individual anatomy," as Held has put it. Obviously this is not only valuable for individual survival but is a necessary requirement if different people are to be able to point to similar things and to discover in common the external regularities. It is a necessary requirement in order to have ostensive definition, so that the very different eyes of the ignorant baby can be counted on as seeing something of the same sort when the mother points with her finger and says, "Light!", and so that shortly the baby is able to point with his finger and to say "Light!" too. And this transcendence of individual anatomy, finally, is what is required if we are to have a public language in which by ostensive definition we can agree on labels and linguistic symbols for the common features we see in the external world. It is satisfying to have a theoretical approach that at last can account for this precise interpersonal transcendence.

The Elimination of Maps

Another feature of this kind of decision-system using functional invariances is that it does not need to contain any "models" or "maps" of the external world. It does not need any little physical models of faces or mountains in the brain, to correspond to those faces and mountains "out there." The supposed maps have been one of the difficulties, I believe, with many analyses of perception. Here is a biological organism, formed of somewhat irregular arrangements of tissue cells, dissimilar to the external milieu and having rather poor connections with it—connections which a learning organism would not know how to interpret at first, anyway. How can such a system form any map of the environment? Or, supposing that it could, who would read it or who would be able to check it? A little homunculus inside? Does he then have to have a brain like ours? And inside his brain, another map of the map? And another smaller homunculus to read that, and so on and on?

I know that there are proponents of this approach who would say that the homunculi—or the clusters of neurons that they represent—just get simpler and simpler, until the last one disappears in a neural pulse or two. But I do not think this has ever been a very satisfactory conclusion, because it gives the highest or most abstract functions the least intelligent control, involving the fewest neurons and the least reliable subsystems. And it does not in any way get around the initial difficulty, which is that, for a learning organism at least, there has never been any way in which the maps could be formed.

I think it is better to try to get away from "maps" entirely and to try to find a model like the one here, which can start without knowing more than some general relations in its built-in core, and which simply goes on searching continually for invariances in its own signal-combinations and self-reinforcing manipulation-loops, organizing and structuring its skill over the environment by progressively structuring itself. I think this gives us, for the first time, a way of bridging the perceptual gap between the dissimilarity of organism and environment, so that in spite of the lack of close coupling and the distortion of inputs and the lack of a map, an organism can still come to transcend its own peculiarities and to "know" its environment and to manipulate it for its own purposes quite successfully.

Time and Space

Another property of a learning decision-system that deserves notice is that its operational time and space are not the time and space of physics, any more than its geometry is the geometry of Euclid. Its inputs are not point particles but extended objects or sensory arrays, and its outputs are not actions at a point but are complex motor manipulations over a region of space. In fact the region of space involved is very ill-defined; the muscles may act on a bone, or a large tool, or they may move a flashlight beam that swings across the horizon for miles.

Likewise, such an organism cannot be said to act at any single point in time. Any output is affected by inputs made at many different times before, and it usually projects forward toward cybernetic or goal-seeking consequences mirrored perhaps by anticipatory invariance-loops within the organism. Where is the instant of time? The loops through the external environment are continuously recycling with different time-constants and have no "instant," no very sharp beginning and no very sharp end. I suspect our idea and our idealization of the "instant" has been developed only because light travels so fast, and the lightning flash can illuminate all our input cells almost at once; but even then our response takes many milliseconds, with different delay-times for sets of muscles in different parts of our bodies.

Obviously any attempt to separate time and space in such a system is artificial. The system is a dynamic system and works on space-time motions and velocities rather than on statics. And in such a system, if it uses functional geometry or some other dynamic-invariance method, there is no such thing as a space relation that can be established independently of a time relation. What is seen in the lightning flash could not have been organized during the flash; the basic regularities had to be learned in times before.

Moreover, in a learning organism, the distinction between structure and operation comes to be blurred, and structure is only time-delayed operation, so to speak. A man's perception or decision depends not only on his inputs of a second ago but on his stored experiences and his parents' accidents and his built-in biological mechanisms developed a million years ago or a hundred million years ago. Where is the instant of time?

Yet, conversely, in a different sense, all this time is here, now, stored in the present system. Operationally, there is no past for a decision-system except what is stored here in the present instant, as nearly as that instant can be defined. There is no future except what is anticipated in the networks or perhaps the goals or extrapolations of the present instant. It is like the rowboat anchored in a flowing river, which may bear the gashes of the past logs that have floated by but which never experiences any part of the river except where it is. In such a system, the only moment of decision and change, the only time there is, is now. It would be an interesting exercise to try to reformulate the usual axiomatic structuring of physics, not using Cartesian space and time, but developing some other formulation in terms of ongoing dynamic processes which have cycles and goals and decisions and stored time instead of separated space and time and discrete points and instants. Such a reformulation might be closer not only to operationalism but to relativity. Like the reformulation of static geometry by functional geometry, it might be not only more "natural" and closer to the biological formulation, but it might also lead to a number of valuable new insights.

Perception as Transaction and Flow

The relations of this kind of decision-system model to its environment must evidently be described, not in static terms, but in terms of ongoing transactions. The psychologists Adelbert Ames and Hadley Cantril have emphasized this transactional nature of perception. If we put the emphasis on operations, there is no clear distinction between "self" and "world" in such a system, as we see in Figure 1. It is true that there may be a fairly sharp boundary between the system and its environment, but operationally the more important entities to be considered are perhaps not the "system" and "environment" so much as the flow-processes that connect them across the boundary, the flow-entities of "awareness" on the input side and of "action" on the output side.

And even this "awareness" and "action" are reafferent, which is to say mixed. An ongoing cycle, from world to self to world and back to self again, has no particular point where it begins or ends; and an imagined cut, not only at the boundary but at any point, would show causal inputs coming in from one side and being checked or reaffirmed by action, and effective outputs going out the other side and being checked or reaffirmed by reafferent stimulation of the inputs. And in emergencies or continuous decision-situations, as in water-skiing or fighting a fire, where the action-time becomes comparable to the judging or invariance-checking time, the boundary not only between self and world but between awareness and action becomes very blurred. Distinctions between the stages of the process, between "awareness" and "action," or between substages such as "awareness," "knowledge," "decision," and "action," can be made only when the operations are slowed down so that these stages and their support loops can begin to be somewhat separated in time.

This kind of transactional flow-situation is of philosophical and linguistic interest because it contrasts so strongly with the static traditional language. The perception of an object by an organism or by this kind of decision-system involves dynamic participation by the organism, interacting with the environment, as the psychologist J. J. Gibson has emphasized. To apply Martin Buber's language to this kind of objective situation, the organism cannot detect an "it" but only an "I-it." Likewise a brain that can interact with another brain through public pointing and linguistic sharing and persuasion and exchange, does not detect a "thou" but an "I-thou" in which its own participation is an essential part of what the other "thou" operationally signifies.

This idea of participative interaction is an insight that goes back a long way in religious and philosophical literature but has been brushed aside by "realists" as being subjective or mystical and nonsensical. But we accept many other subjective insights, and I believe that the real reason for this rejection of the more accurate transactional picture of perception is that the objective signs of the dynamic interaction are so small and subtle. They are confined to little things like eye movements which were forced by evolution to be inconspicuous, for the survival of both predators and prey. This is why men have been able to build up and keep the simple static picture of perception for so long. Such a picture is evidently a close and useful approximation for ordinary objective purposes, but it leads to a static and passive language, of "self" and "world" and "I" and "see" and "it," designed to shut out transactional or time-space or flow ideas which contradict it.

The transactional relation of an organism to its environment is something like Robert Heinlein's earthworm who met another earthworm and said, "You're beautiful. Will you marry me?" And the other earthworm said, "Don't be silly. I'm your other end."

This story perhaps illustrates the difficulty of perception in an environment where there is no visual field! But it is also intended to illustrate the idea that everything we meet—or more objectively, everything a decision-network meets—whether a human being, a stray cat, a flower, or a rock, is the other side of a feedback loop of our learning and storage system, is in some sense our cousin under creation—is in some sense our other end.

Amplification and Manipulation

Another aspect of a transaction-making decision-system that should not be forgotten is that it is by its nature an amplifying system, or more exactly, a selecting-and-amplifying-and-manipulating system operating on the environment around it. A living system not only draws in energy and material supplies from the environment, but it uses them in an amplified and self-maintaining reaction on the environment—a reaction carefully selected so as to keep these supplies flowing in. To accomplish this, particular input patterns are very specifically selected, and they are then amplified, often by factors of millions or more, to produce a highly specific output with a specific and effective grasp reaching out into selected parts of the environment. Needless to say, this kind of manipulation may change the environment drastically. A sensory-motor decision-system alters everything around it, and its effects, desired or not, propagate indefinitely. Seeds are put in; the prairies are planted; the forests are leveled; the earth's magnetic field is shaken by man's experiments. A selected and altered future is continually branching out indefinitely from the vicinity of any decision-system. It is easy to see that, in such a vicinity, the difficulty of detailed causal predictions of the outcome from outside observations of the local and subtle combinations of the original inputs is very great, and in fact it may be greater than the difficulty implied by any indeterminacy we know in physics or atomic theory.

Scientific Knowledge and Cybernetic Knowledge

In fact, by observing the interaction between a decision-system and its environment, one sees particularly clearly the relation between scientific knowledge and what might be called the cybernetic or operation-knowledge of the organism. Scientific knowledge is relatively passive knowledge, what the organism observes in its environment with relatively little interaction. Cybernetic knowledge is active knowledge, where the organism makes large or manipulative interactions with the environment. We have "weak interaction" with objects in observing them, "strong interaction" in manipulating them.

The ideal of science is that kind of observer-free world—or half-world—that is called an "isolated system," like the top half of Figure 1, a system which we can prepare and then take our hand away from, so as to see how this "objective" system will behave as it moves "by itself." This is not quite possible—even physics says there cannot be observation without some interaction—but it is what makes classical determinism a good approximation.

But the purpose of human knowledge, or the knowledge gained or invariances stored by a decision-system, is the wiser guidance of action, to desired ends. "Scientific detachment" has been a most powerful tool for understanding the environment. But the organism should not take it for an end; it should not blind us to the bottom half of Figure 1 or the relations between the halves. The real purpose of detachment is better directed involvement. This is a cybernetic purpose, with "strong interaction," as men manipulate objects at every instant to direct them closer to goals. To overstate it a little, physics is the science of weak-interaction, of determinism or indeterminism, on *that* side of the boundary; whereas cybernetics is the science of strong-interaction, of will, of human purpose, of applied knowledge, on *this* side of the boundary.

Scientific detachment has its value in determining more clearly how the universe works, but it does not stop there. We see, not merely from looking at ourselves, but from examining these other objective decision-systems and models, that the purpose of scientific detachment is to make commitment and choice more intelligent; to make decisions suit our purposes better; and to make scientific involvement more effective.

INTERPRETATION OF THE SUBJECTIVE

Validating the Objective

All this finally brings us full circle to the point where we are prepared to ask whether these objective experiments and current conceptual models of how brains operate can help us to understand and interpret our own subjective experiences or can give us a better language for describing them. That is, we can ask, as we asked with eyeballs, are these *our* brains?

I believe that, in broad outline, at least, the answer is Yes. In the first place, this model of our own brain operation appears to be self-consistent—as it was designed to be. This is another example of a self-consistent and self-reinforcing loop. In the course of our argument, we have now gone in a great circle from the world of objects talked about, to a scientific model within that world, and now back by analogy to see if the model can account for the main features of our subjective experience, and so, if it does, to the validation of our subjective observation-creation of the world of objects again. I think it is clear that we can indeed confirm in our own experience what the model says about how we, as decision-networks, might have constructed and are still constructing our objective world, our public world, of objects and people and language and science.

Can we see the need for eyeball-motion in our own vision? Yes, by putting on the Ditchburn or Riggs apparatus. Can we see the value of self-motion in giving three-dimensional depth? Yes, by moving our heads. Are the regularities of objects those of an external public space as functional geometry indicates? Yes, we can talk about them with the other people-objects.

In the development of language, do we not act like a learning, manipulating, reafferent-feedback model? Yes, we can remember or empathize with how a baby follows lights, and traces objects and faces, and sees eyes and fingers pointing, and hears mouths saying, "Light, light! See the light!"—and how a few months later he makes the same noises himself. We all go on learning the names of new objects and people by this same ostensive process every day, continually validating our participation in the common language community. We see that our objective world has been built up simultaneously with the "I-thou" interactions of language. The objects and people all become named objects, pointed to, played with, and defined operationally and linguistically. Finally the language itself becomes "transparent" to us, as Suzanne Langer has emphasized; we think objects and ideas, not words—until a bilingual person quoting a conversation may not even remember which language he was talking.

We also act like a manipulating decision-network as we make the childish beginnings of objective science and so complete the validation of the objective. We remember or reconfirm, day after day, that the chair bumps and the knife cuts and that two bodies cannot be in the same place at the same time. We roll a ball, that perfect Galilean and Newtonian object, and it teaches without a teacher, showing over and over to the two-year old child things about free bodies moving in a straight line that even philosophers had not clearly formulated five hundred years ago. (It is another self-reinforcing loop, from the seers to society and back to the young seers, who find the scientific concepts more self-evident in every generation.)

Our closure of the object-model-subjective loop by validation is a necessary step. The subjective has to validate the objective, or everything is nonsense. Schrödinger quotes a fragment from Democritus in which the intellect has an argument with the senses about what is "real." The intellect says, like an objective atomic physicist, "Ostensibly there is color, ostensibly sweetness, ostensibly bitterness, actually only atoms and void." To which the senses retort, "Poor intellect, do you hope to defeat us while from us you borrow your evidence? Your victory is your defeat." If we allow the senses to be manipulative, to be not passive awareness only but awareness-and-action, this evidently would be the view of the perception psychologists as well as existentialists today.

Physical Science and the Primary Reality

Where in this approach is the "objective" physical world of Newton's laws and Dalton's atoms and Rutherford's nuclei? It is evidently in a simplified subsection of *our* subjective totality, subject to *our* decision as to whether we find it useful to believe in these atoms or not.

But are not the atoms, or the other fundamental particles of which the universe is supposed to be made, the realest things there are? Even within the framework of physical science there has always been some doubt. Ostwald and other great experimental chemists of the last century never thought that atoms were real. They said, as Laplace said of God, that "they had no need of that hypothesis." And our atoms today may dissolve at any moment into interferences of waves traveling at the speed of light or into some other bizarre reformulation, just as the Bohr orbits of 1912 dissolved into Schrödinger waves and then into Heisenberg matrices, more for reasons of elegance and unity than for any great improvement in prediction. I think this raises some serious questions for those who believe in physical science as the foundation of the world. What kind of primary reality is this, whose elements depend so much on time and taste, in successive new approximations to an ultimate description that they never reach?

Oh, atoms are real enough in an operational sense; we make television sets and bombs with their reality. We break our bones against their bonds, as Samuel Johnson showed. But it is the operations that are real; the atoms and the bonds are only a secondary reality that we have derived, or invented—a reality that must take its evidence, its confirmation, and its meaning from the true primary reality of our experiences, our manipulations, and our changing human choices and linguistic formulations. It is *our* experience that proves that stones are hard and have certain X-ray patterns, not the explanation that they are made of special atoms or bonds. Find a soft stone, and the physical theory will have to accommodate itself to restate that fact for you! Physics is a useful and magnificent slave, but still a slave; and let us not forget it. It is slave philosophy to tell us that he, Physics, is the primary reality. We must never mistake the approximations for the whole, or the derived for the real, or the tool for the creative hand.

This point of view therefore rejects the primacy of the "naive realism" of objects, and it rejects as well the primacy of the scientific and atomic inferences and explanations used for describing the objective world. It asserts, rather, the primacy of the subjective experience and perceptions from which (by inference from the models) the objective world "originally" had to be derived or constructed by the organism, and without whose accuracy and "transcendence" this objective world would be unreliable. It is clear that Democritus, moving from objective physics to subjective validation, was a forerunner of Mach, Bridgman, Schrödinger, and Bohm.

Each reader or hearer, of course, can only appreciate the full force of these arguments and of this shift of viewpoint if he treats these arguments, not as relating to the print on the paper or some objective external brain or organism such as another person or the dog by the fire, but as relating to himself. For each of you, I would hope that your immediate primary reality is not anything so speculative and so difficultly verifiable as the fundamental particles and motions of physics, but rather your immediate present totality of experience, the sensations you are now experiencing and your thoughts about what you are reading or what else you wish you were doing right now. Think that the primary reality is anything else or anywhere else, whether in physics or in heaven or in an afterlife, and you damage the accuracy and quality and humanity of your perceptions. "Subjective validation" means you, the reader, (or I, the author) looking out at these written words, this diagram, these objects around you or me—and deciding whether the primary reality should be attributed to these objects or, instead, to our perception of them. Doubt that you are seeing them right, and you doubt everything.

The objective world of the physical sciences is only half a world. It contains nothing that is really and humanly important to us as feeling and thinking physiological beings, no love and no vomiting, no thrills, no memories, no plans, no ideas, no human interaction and creation, and no death.

And if we interpret the word "primary" to mean the original

processes by which a human baby learns about the world, it is clear that the primary reality for us even at that stage surely cannot be physics or the atoms. It is the mother's arms, the mother's nipple, that gives the baby his first external contact with that human-interacting ever-loving world that generates us, feeds us, shares its life with us, and makes us all a part of evolution and the human continuity. And what I mean by the mother's nipple is of course the whole system of family and social care. I mean by it in particular what might be thought of as the "intellectual nipple" of mankind —the mother's voice speaking the mother language which teaches us and transfers to us the first collective human symbols for our philosophers of science to analyze and manipulate. Without the mother's voice, without that ostensive definition that is the mother's finger pointing to the light, to the red ball, to the toy, to the baby sister, where would these symbols be that we manipulate with our semantic-linguistic philosophy? The reality on which all later discourse about reality depends is this reality of a language which so incredibly *can* be ostensively agreed upon between adult and baby, can be shared and can be taught to us by other human beings, and which therefore transcends our personal individuality and makes it possible for us to discuss these more abstract problems of physics or philosophy. The ultimate philosophical basis of physics cannot be understood without first understanding those perception-theory aspects of the totality that make such a remarkable phenomenon possible.

So even in the cradle we see that there already must be the beginnings of many of the components we find in our personal primary reality as adults: I-it awareness and I-thou human nourishment, sharing-teaching, and language.

This approach also gives us a new understanding of "operationalism" in the physical sciences. Physics has often been spoken of and idealized as "operational," meaning that the only realities we know in physics are the operational, testable realities. "What will happen if I do this?"—for example, if I drop this pencil—*that* is the subject matter of physics. A reminder of this viewpoint has been the healthy corrective of many windy theories. But in this technological society, as one might imagine, it is only the objective side of operationalism that has been singled out for emphasis. The very term "operationalism," which originally emphasized action, manipulation, choice, has often come to be identified simply with detached phenomenology or the raw collection of facts. A fuller operationalism, with fuller attention to motives and choice, might lead us to a more analytical consideration of hypotheses and inferences as well as to more consideration of the other, subjective, aspects of the operation—of whether I *want* to drop the pencil or *should* drop it or whether I am convinced afterward that I understand the experiment or that the theory fits it adequately.

This is where the personal enters into mathematics and science, as L. J. Savage has emphasized. The existential fact is that it is we who choose the problems and it is we who must be convinced by the proof. The bases of these choices and convictions often hide in the scientific unconscious, perhaps because we do not want to feel that there is a choice; it might be healthier if we brought the choices into the open. For it is at these crucial points of initiation and conclusion that intelligence, values, and purposes make their very personal entry into science and serve, or fail to serve, our larger human needs. I believe that a fuller operationalism viewed, as Bridgman viewed it, within the personal-perceptual framework I have described, would make the personal nature of our scientific choices clearer and might straighten out many subconscious and pathological knots in our teaching and research practices and our service to society.

In operationalism, man is the operator, you are the operator, I am the operator. But it is important to see in addition that our every act branches out to our own new operations which are themselves unpredictable. We shape the world anew at every moment. The reason these operations are unpredictable is that they are not a part of objective science. Our precursor states and causal chains are not accessible to us in the form of data. "By quantum mechanics it is impossible for an observer to determine his own wavefunction; observations on your own mind are not data," said Leo Szilard. Such observations do not constitute material for any causal or deterministic prediction, because the "observer" interacts too strongly with the thing observed or predicted and can falsify any prediction by choosing to do exactly the opposite. The result is that the future shaped by human beings is not the determinate Minkowski space of relativity physics, a "frozen passage" with frozen time, but, as the philosopher Milič Čapek has emphasized, a future in process of becoming, freely restructured by the thinking mind at every moment.

Powers and Dangers of Language

It is worth digressing a moment to see that this view of the objective world, as learned by manipulating it functionally and by shared ostensive naming, gives us a basis for analyzing the role of words in our perceptual organization. It is surprising how large a

part words play in helping us to manipulate the objective world
successfully—or in keeping us from it. Words begin, of course, as
small parts of the objective world. They are both objects and actions; sound objects and mouth actions, print objects and hand actions. And when they have been ostensibly defined by pointing,
they come to denote other objects and actions.

Yet it is obvious that denotation is not the principal value of
words. If it were, it would be no more than a child's game to call
them out when you saw something. But calling-out and naming
leads to chanting and verbal memory when a thing is elsewhere,
and to expectation, and verbal memory of long ago, and perception
of consequences, and planning. To our amplifying and manipulating systems, these small signs and muscular actions can signal and
symbolize and finally can initiate larger actions. This is their power,
that they make it possible, with little expenditure of energy, first, to
discuss alternatives in quick sequence—what is not here as well as
what is—and, second, to telescope in a moment our past action and
future action-consequences, without having to carry out the larger
acts or wait for the results.

Where did the ball go? Where will I find it? What are you
going to do? Day after day the child practices talking about what is
not there, until by the time he is four or six, he has become a
"time-binding animal." He can discuss intelligently the finishing of
the building or the flight around the world or where he lived when
he was two or the best way to do things.

But as long-range choosing and planning become habitual,
there comes not only the transparency of language but also what
could be called the "objectification" of thought. We see in our
mind's eye the scale of numbers and the ladder of time. The distant
world, the past and future, may become more real to us than what
is before our eyes. How this is hooked into the anticipation-loops
that we call visual and emotional imagination is not yet clear, but
when we hear a story, we do not hear just the sound of the words,
as perhaps a dog might hear them; we are *there* with Archimedes or
with the boys in the cave. We read the newspaper and we do not
see the sunshine or the people in the bus, but only the black happenings of the war.

And these words are not emotionally neutral. Objectification
means that emotionally, they *are* the objects—and were from the
beginning. They symbolize; they are "secondary reinforcers," as the
psychologist B. F. Skinner says. So they get coupled into our biochemical loops and our strong behavior.

This has great benefits and great dangers. When the words are true and the emotions appropriate, we can be motivated to build the Ark before the rain starts falling. This emotional power is what brings us all together in collective fear and collective hope and determination and makes it possible to undertake vast enterprises. Even the small lies of a fictional story may be valuable in showing us a deeper truth, in broadening our human sympathies and in teaching us things we need to know about hardship and courage and the ways of love.

The danger is that the words may be large lies, not true in any sense. Words are so weakly coupled to the objects and actions they denote that it is mechanically as easy to talk lies and nonsense as it is to talk truth. This can lead us into catastrophe; and the result is that we have to be strongly reinforced against these lies and mistakes. We have to make up rules and laws to choose the word-combinations that symbolize our action-consequences correctly. We devise grammar, logic, the rules of objective truth, and the laws of science. (Action cannot lie; action is. It is words that give us alternatives, lies, and laws.)

So we ask for confirmation and for crucial experiments in the courts and in the laboratory. We often punish the lie or the alien view more strongly than crime. The contradiction cuts across the community of perception. It warns that something has gone wrong with the reinforcement-loops, with our collective reality-testing mechanism. We know not what black thing hides in the darkness. As a result, men have often bought confirmation with the group at the expense of confirmation with nature—although in the long run this bargain always leads to disastrous results.

Yet we run into a far more insidious danger, individually and collectively, when we make emotional identifications with words that are not merely lies but are empty of *any* meaning, true or false, for decision and action—that is, words that are empty of operational referents or of any testable reality at all. Lies we can refute, but we can never come to grips with twisted words.

Is not this the source of many of our neurotic problems? We invent, and are obsessed by, verbal hopes and hates and fears when there is nothing tangible there. We come to hate unreal collectives, like racial or national groups. We are obsessed by guilt or by endless striving, as we still try to satisfy or avoid the childhood demands of parents or an angry God. We go over and over the choices we might have made, losing the ones we can still make. We are obsessed by thoughts of death, rather than making the most of life. Our ambitions are verbal ambitions, to "catch up," to outdo the others; or gambling ambitions, to win or to be picked out of the crowd—ambitions that keep receding and can never be really satisfied.

Probably most, if not all, of our strong and persistent emotions and rigidities are persistent precisely because they are aimed at verbal and unreal goals that have, in all human probability, no meaning we could ever meet or be satisfied with. We wait for the glass slipper and never learn to dance. We poison our evenings with success and what we get is ulcers. It never lets up, because it is inside.

The Subjective as Participant

On the other hand, a decision-system that is acting effectively is not only coupled to its real world, it almost becomes one with it. Is it not so with us? When we pick up or name even so common an object as a pencil, we are *participating* with the pencil in a process thick with history. It is not just that our eyes must scan the pencil or our fingers must trace it in order to see it or know it; it is that the whole perception, and its significance and testing, involves a complex participation-process we have stored—a process that extends back into remembered and unremembered childhood, with our parents practicing with us, and correcting our pointing and naming, for many a pencil and person and thing. And no doubt it involves *their* childhood and adulthood and how they learned the language and were culturally structured to care for a baby and teach it.

And of course our perception of a person is far more participative than our perception of a pencil. Any perception of those information-rich and responsive and unpredictable objects that we call human beings is "I-thou" overwhelmingly. Just in a blank stare or the lift of a shoulder, we read purposes and values, criticisms and praise and cooperative effort. When we listen to each other, we hear not air pulses but words, not words but meanings, images, threats, plans.

And today we know that we even have an "I-thou" relation to the rest of the universe as well—a developmental and evolutionary transactional relationship. Our structures and attitudes are shaped by a father and mother who gave us heredity and milk and education. But they are shaped in a larger and deeper sense by the world around us that has shaped our living molecules. Our life is something that grew up out of the primordial molecules and dust under the sun's radiation, and perhaps it makes in us some progress toward more intelligence and brains. We are children of the universe, even objective science now says, in some sense destined and designed to be here and to be aware—and to be interested in perception problems.

So we move in a kinship field. When we look out at the molecules and aggregates that we rearrange in our factories or grow on our farms, we are looking at our cousins. The pigments in our eyes can respond to the colors of the pigments of leaves and flesh only because they are chemically similar molecules. As Pascal said, "Man . . . is related to all he knows. . . . He is in a dependent alliance with everything." And Emerson, more modern, said,

> He is not only representative, but participant. Like can only be known by like. . . . Man, made of the dust of the world, does not forget his origin. . . . Thus we sit by the fire and take hold on the poles of the earth.

The Subjective as Manipulant

I think the decision-system model of our minds also confirms this deeper insight of Emerson's—the realization that our perception-process goes over continuously into our larger manipulation of the world around us. We do not often think of perception as manipulation, because the brain somehow organizes our ever-changing visual observation-fields into a continuous seen-and-remembered "stable world," and because simple passive observation, even with moving eyeballs, changes the objects and relations of this "stable world" very little, so that we think of it as unaffected by our observation; but manipulation it is, nevertheless, manipulation by the electrical signals in the outgoing nerves, by the motion of the eyeballs, and finally by the hands. "Knowledge is action," as Skinner says. Perception of the world is only delayed action; or, more exactly, it is a weak-action prelude to delayed strong-action, the first step toward the shaping of the world. A decision-system always amplifies its energies, first in perceiving and then in modifying the environment around it; and man is the most spectacular example. It is increasingly a world that we have seen, studied, and shaped ourselves. The time-constants extend from an instant ago to years ago and centuries and millenniums ago.

Thus, I now realize that when I see a pencil, I know it is there only because I manipulated its image a fraction of a second ago. But then I place it on the table with tactile manipulation. Does it surprise me that it is there? No; it would surprise me if it were not, and I would doubt my perception. I look away for several seconds, but am I not still manipulating it?—for I expect to see it, and perhaps to pick it up again, if I look back. Is this any different in principle from expecting to see my car in the street where I left it—manipulated it—an hour ago? Or the line of trees my father planted on the farm? Or the new subdivision I have read about in the newspaper?

Today the scope of this perception-extrapolation-manipulation by man is almost incredible. It is hard to walk in a city and see any line or object that man has not shaped, except where he deliberately allows some natural variation, as with grass or trees. It is hard to see any plant or animal that he has not bred or any landscape that he has not changed. Even the variations in the sky and sea are partly his and may some day be under his control. We are not only sons of the earth, we are participants and builders of it. As Emerson says again, "The world becomes at last only a realized will—the double of the man." It is a tool responding to our decision-systems, almost as much "I-thou" as the bones in our fingers.

The great extent of this participation-manipulation-prediction leads to an unexpected realization about the degree of our involvement with the world. In the past, some philosophers have talked of analyzing perception in terms of two elements, the "given" and the "not-given," or the "for-itself (*pour-soi*)" and the "in-itself (*en-soi*)," thinking of these as primitives from which could be derived (by interaction between them) whatever is correct about our usual picture of objects and of the subjective field. The "given" is largely the objective part, and is the "surprising" or "absurd" aspect, because we (the "not-given") did not anticipate or intend it.

But I believe that this view, at least in its extreme form, is derived from the static fallacy of perception. We see from the present analysis that there is in fact no sharp boundary between the "given" and the "not-given." In fact, it is surprising how little is "given" to us, instant by instant and hour by hour, how little is truly "surprising," when we know what we are manipulating and where we have put things and what men have done. A decision-system like man manipulates and stores. Its memories are expectations. Its steady-state loops extend into the environment. And as a result the environment constantly becomes more docile and less surprising, more and more an intimate part of the decision-system itself.

Naming the Subjective

These perception-relations we have been describing are simple, however, compared to the aspects of the subjective which we must now discuss and which have always been sources of puzzlement and contradiction. I refer to the problem of naming the subjective, and the problems of time and the self and the uniqueness of consciousness and the change of attitude with subjective realization. And here again, although I do not wish to be dogmatic about it, I think the decision-system model offers some helpful analogies and clarifications.

In discussions of subjective perception, one of the central problems has always been the difficulty of trying to name and talk about the whole subjective field, because of the impossibility of making ostensive definitions of such a thing. The modern mathematician, however, can speak accurately of classes, sets, and fields, and many other concepts of things that cannot be pointed to.

I believe that today we can use the same method in describing the perceptual field. I think we can talk quite accurately not only of objects that can be pointed to at a given moment, but of sets of such objects, and of the whole visual field—the "V-field"—containing these objects at a given moment. (Perhaps the number of possible different objects in such a field, if we had infinite resolution, would in fact be comparable to the mathematician's number, *Aleph-Two*, which is the number of all the possible curves in a plane.)

I think we can also go on to talk of a second, larger field, the field of all our sensations at a given moment—the "S-field." We now realize, of course, that the sensations we are aware of are not something static, but must have been compounded of sensory inputs varied by motor operations, with reafferent-stimulation and time delays, and constant checking and what could be called "veridification" of the field. (By veridification is meant the process of checking whether the perceived relations in the field are veridical and self-consistent.)

But finally, and in the same way, I think we can talk fairly accurately of a still larger field, the field of the totality of all our subjective experience at a given moment. This might be called the "totality-field"—the "T-field"—and it would include not only the sensation-field, but all the memories, emotions, expectations, and so on of which we are aware. The fact that such a field cannot be pointed to does not make it impossible to discuss accurately, any more than the fact that the infinity of all the possible curves in a plane cannot be pointed to. And within this totality-field, these other elements which are not part of what we may call immediate sensation or action—elements such as memories, emotions, and so on—may still have operational definition, both subjective and objective. For we may show them in our voluntary or involuntary muscular or biochemical expression, or in talking about them; and we can see their effects in shaping the speed and style of our action.

I think this is much like the world we should expect a learning decision-network to have (as suggested in Figure 1). Whatever its inputs, it experiences or acts on the totality of them. And those features that are stored in its strucutre and history are still detectable, by reafferent signals, from their effects on its output.

In fact, it is interesting to reflect that the world of each decision-network and of each creature is probably always "complete." The span of perception is "full" in every coordinate. The field of perception is total and has no "holes" in it. Or, as Mach says, in commenting on our own blind spots, which we cannot see directly, "A defect of light-sensation can no more be noticed at a point blind from the beginning than the blindness, say, of the skin of the back can cause a gap in the visual field." This is what we expect with an invariant-selecting system.

So, no doubt, if we could ever learn the subjective responses of an earthworm, or a fish, or a dog, we should find that their perceptual field seems to them to be sharp, clear, complete, rapidly changing, and interesting, just as ours does to us. They do not see what we see, no; but it is not perceived as an incompleteness, any more than our inability to hear the echoes of the bats is perceived as an incompleteness, or a child's inability to understand the financial transactions of his father. It is something that might be added; but surely we are all incomplete and ignorant children with respect to the added patterns that still lie ahead.

Time and the Eternal Now

I believe that the decision-network model is especially helpful in considering the subjective problem of time. Subjective time, when we think about it, has several odd aspects not expressed in our usual objective language. It seems to me, for example, that subjectively we do not sharply separate time and space, any more than a decision-network does. I suspect that "now" is never merely "now" for us, but something more like "now-all-this-changing."

In addition, we can see for ourselves that it is not an instantaneous now, but a spreading fuzzy now that integrates influences from a second ago and hours ago and years ago, and from anticipation-loops whose trains are set in motion for times ahead. It is an ongoing, space-processing, ever-changing, relation-seeking now. Not a now of statics, but of time-derivatives and velocities. I often think it would be good if we could replace our usual static nouns and is-verbs by the "-ing" noun forms and continuing-action verb forms of English, just to keep us reminded of this continuing relationing. "I see the red flower" should perhaps be translated to something with a more dynamic and oriental flavor, such as "Seeing red-reflecting flowering in space-near-me-ing."

Yet the most evident feature and the one least represented in our usual language is that all time is present together in this Now. We objectify the time of dates and memories and plans, but the re-membering and planning is now. All time and space that is opera-tionally real to us and actionable is present to us here and now, however diffuse this now may be. The storage in the network, or the feedback anticipation loops, are present storage and present loops. Anything that is not stored is not remembered; operationally in the present, it has not been. However much we may enjoy order-ing and remembering the past and however much the scholars may try to make it more orderly and objective for us, "the only time there is, is now," as lovers say, and water-skiers, and preachers of conversion.

Of course, it is hard to pull most Westerners away from some-how "identifying" with the objectification of time. We see ourselves as "then" or "there." This kind of objectification is easy and valua-ble in verbal and analytical goal analysis. It helps us plan when to start supper and how long the trip will take, and to imagine what we will do next summer. Planning and ethics become long-range and goal-directed. This is the great verbal and moral achievement that words and clocks and calendars have given us. But when we look at nothing but this verbal and objectified future all the time, we lose sight of the non-verbal real and present around us, often in-deed the very thing that our past goals were reaching for.

With such an attitude, any satisfying attainment is forever im-possible. I think that we should recognize the value of objectifica-tion and use it; but when we have gone too far in this direction, it would be a gain if we could come back more often, especially in our personal relations, to the immediate and real. Many large and good schemes fail because they are only paper schemes and objectified schemes; they are separated from effectiveness because they do not start from any personal transactional good in the immediate pres-ent. We are active manipulating decision-systems; and it is the vari-ety and richness and responsiveness of our immediate contacts with the world that make our amplifications directed and powerful.

I hope that perhaps our attitudes today may be changing toward a more existential sense of immediacy. The girl writes on the wall, "There is no tomorrow, Tolin. So how about this afternoon?"

Blunt, shameless, but true. Seize the day. What more effective long-range program could she have planned? The future starts here. This is the objectification of a very different time-attitude, the attitude of living in an ever-changing, timeless moment that contains all time (just as the spaceless visual field, which cannot be pointed to, contains all space). This is the eternal Now of love and action—not the old objectified kind of future eternity that was supposed to come by working and waiting, but a change of perspective that you can start at any moment, as instantly as breathing. With such an attitude, we can feel our intimate and personal and responsive involvement continually starting the most effective causal chains branching out indefinitely into an ever-altered environment and an ever-changing future. The action-moment of the decision-network ceases to be the deterministic "frozen passage" of the old physical relativity theory and becomes a moment of continually new interacting and becoming and shaping, as Henri Bergson said, and as Milič Čapek emphasizes.

Elimination of the Self

Many of the elements that we can study in objective models and decision-networks naturally and necessarily drop out of our subjective fields. As we have noted, the detailed structure of the retina cannot be seen, or the shadows of the blood vessels or the distortion of the images. Perception transcends anatomy. It is designed for manipulating the external world. Our networks are not programmed to see these uncorrected sensory inputs, but to see invariances and external relationships.

We are also largely unaware of the second-stage elements, such as our invariance-selecting processes and our small feedback loops from manipulation to reafferent stimulation. They may define the boundaries of objects and determine the veridicality of space-relations, but we have learned to talk objectively about public "objects" "themselves" and to ignore these rapid common actions that generate them for us. And it is only when we move slowly that we can even separate the reafferent awareness-loops from the reefferent action-loops. Both of them are flow-transactions and feedback-transactions across the boundary between "self" and "world"; and the boundary is also something that is not present in perception.

Though we may see this boundary in an objective system, we have no sense organs to see it in our subjective one, any more than we can see our own eyes.

But what seems to generate the most operational confusion and the most hard words in perception arguments is that the decision-network itself also does not appear in the subjective perception. We have no eyes to see it either. In the subjective totality-field there is no object or class of objects or of actions that can be pointed to or isolated as "self" or "ego" or "I." In any observation or operation, there is no sharp distinction between the manipulating and the manipulated. The "self" and the "world" as commonly spoken of, are seen to be inseparably blended when we examine any experiences closely. Without manipulation, there are no objects to manipulate; without objects to manipulate, there is no reference point and no manipulation. Likewise, on the awareness side, there is no extracting without acting, and no acting without extracting. These are self-reinforcing loops; and they cease to be loops at all if either leg is missing. So, operationally, there *are* objects; but "I" am the operating. Objects are the nouns of which we are the verbs. Nouns without verbs are grammatically and operationally meaningless, "like the sound of one hand clapping." More exactly, we are the totality-verb that encompasses all the other verbs. In this sense, it is we who give objects existence; we are the "is."

This merging of the self into the world seems startling when first reflected upon. Yes, it is obvious, but we are not taught it. In fact, we train it out of the child, and our mature linguistic usage contradicts it—as medieval usage about "motion" contradicted the idea of continued motion in a straight line. And we rarely examine our own immediate experience to see how misleading the linguistic usage is. But consider your own case now. Where is the "self?" Are you not involved in everything you see or feel? If so, why make this artificial separation, speaking of the "self" as though it were another noun?

Evidently we pick up the "self"-words, and pronouns about ourselves, as object-words from other people, as we discuss each other's independence of decision. But this "self" is, if anything, a diffuse choosing-center or, better, an active verb, and not a body that can be pointed to, even by other people; and it has no separate representation in any aspect of our own perceptual field. The grammatical separation of the subject from the verb has made it seem to be an object, but perhaps we should reunite them again, as in Latin. I-choose, I-go, would be a less misleading way to talk of decision-ing and action-ing and interaction-ing. Each of us can say for himself: "I" am the totality-verb of acting-manipulating-creating-and-invarianting the self-and-environment.

The Uniqueness of Consciousness

A related oddity of the subjective field that has also led to extensive linguistic and philosophical disagreement is its aspect of uniqueness. For a decision-system, and for us, consciousness is always undivided and unending. Or as Schrödinger says, "Consciousness is never experienced in the plural, only in the singular," and within it there is no awareness of a beginning or an end. We do prefix it with the word "my," because we admit there are other people and other decision-systems. But no matter how many of us there are, there is only one subjective consciousness involved in any operation, just as there is only one flowerpot on this table. It is true that we see the flowerpot from many points of view, and talk about their differences—but it might equally well be said that we experience "the consciousness" from many points of view.

Because of this operational similarity, it might be less confusing if we said "my view of the consciousness," just as we say "my view of the flowerpot." Or we could do the opposite, and drop the word "view" in both cases and say only *"my* flowerpot" because it is in *"my* consciousness." It is interesting to note that either of these attempts at parallel treatment is generally regarded as mystical and unsound by "realists." They learned to say *"the* flowerpot" and *"my* consciousness" at their mother's knee. So they feel that any personalizing of the flowerpot is dangerous; and, conversely, that any reduction of their consciousness to just a "view" of something universal threatens to blend their own self-image and separate value into something larger—as indeed it does.

But I would claim that it is just as possible linguistically and quite legitimate operationally to speak of our various perception fields as being no more "personal" than the various views of the world that we see in mirrors at different angles. Is it not possible that there are mutual regularities in our joint perception that transcend the individual views? I think it is, and I think this is what Schrödinger was asserting in his curious "Epilogue," where he starts operationally from this *singulare tantum,* this singularity of consciousness. We have now seen transcendence over and over, how our perceptual invariances transcend anatomy and how our social invariances of truth and of concepts transcend our own individual irregularities. We find that we are pattern-perceiving, regularity-reinforcing, world-invarianting creatures, individually and collectively. The result is that your invariant, if well-observed, may be equivalent to mine, or to that of an ancient sage or a future one. As Thoreau says,

> The oldest Egyptian or Hindu philosopher raised a corner of the veil. . . . I gaze upon as fresh a glory as he did, since it was I in him that was then so bold, and it is he in me that now reviews the vision. . . . No time has elapsed since that divinity was revealed.

Thoreau identified himself with a single consciousness growing across the ages, whose growth-points or realization-points contributed a single realization, no matter what individual body or what century they were in. In view of today's intellectual convergence, it is not a bad view to adopt, nor an impossible one.

The Jump of Realization

I believe this all leads us to a more accurate and satisfying subjective view than our usual language has given us. It is a view in which "awareness" is a totality-field, "now" is an ongoing immediacy that contains all time, "self" and "world" are a mixed pair that cannot be separated, "objects" are an interaction-invariance extraction, and "I" is an acting verb. These would be natural usages for a decision-network. If we talked more often in these terms, it might help to recover our sense of the subjective as the total immediate interacting present. It would help us to keep straight the proper relations between subjective and objective. The subjective is the primitive and direct experience out of which the objective is drawn, the experience from which all our partial and analytical and passive and detached notions, our ideas of far-away and past and future, are derived. And it is the subjective that has emotions and values and purposes and knowledge and decisions and acts, the purposes that these abstractions are made to serve.

These are not new insights, although the present derivation in terms of modern experiments and models may be new. Rather, they are ideas that are old in human history, ideas that many a primitive savage understands better than a civilized man, but that have become taboo to discuss today, almost more taboo than sex. Are you not made uncomfortable at trying to talk scientifically about the subjective? Where is the source of this emotional discomfort? In our modern objectivism we are embarrassed to talk about such subjects, about "awareness" or "self" or the "I," either in the family or in scientific journals. Only preachers and poets are allowed to discuss such matters—and they are permitted only because we do not be-

lieve them anyway, and we neither want to nor have to answer
them back. And when thinkers and philosophers in the Western
world have made statements like the ones here, which seem to deny
the primacy of the objective or which put the emphasis on a subjective operationalism, this has caused them to be rejected as solipsists
and mystics—as Bridgman and Schrödinger have been rejected—
although they always insisted that *they* were the true realists. It
seems to me that the present type of derivation through objective
models permits us to bridge this gap much more peaceably, in a
self-consistent loop that permits many starting-points, so that we can
see the value and truth of each type of insight in its proper field.

It is true that in the past, the attempt to get away from the derived and to practise a new directness, a subjective or an existential
directness, has been a rare experience. It is like the realization of
the constancy of motion in a straight line, which was, because of the
linguistic and conceptual barrier, a relatively rare experience before
Galileo. As a result, the realization of the primacy of the subjective
has not usually been something taught to children but has been
rather an adult Gestalt-insight, a complete jump of perspective
which came with the force of revelation.

Such Gestalt-jumps are familiar to us from the examples in elementary psychology texts, such as the "staircase" outline which most
people can acquire the knack of "flipping," so that it is seen either
as a perspective view from above or as a view from below. We can
make a similar flip in interchanging the roles of figure and ground
—the faces and the vase—in certain drawings. And there is a far
more remarkable flip in the "inversion" of the three-dimensional
staircase-figures and other figures studied by Mach and more recently by Murray Eden and by Cyril Smith at M.I.T. Many people
have trouble making these three dimensional inversions, but when
they do, the "Aha!" reaction and the sense of surprise and delight
are dramatic, and they may go on for hours studying the strange
properties and reversed movements of the inverted forms.

Is it any wonder that the complete flip from the ordinary
objective view to a realization of the primacy and inclusiveness of
the subjective—involving as it does the whole world-outlook—
might cause a similar surprise and delight and an ongoing exploration which one could never stop talking about? Or that these excla-
mations of surprise might cause a similar bafflement and derision in
those who have not made the flip?

When the flip has come, it has often come like a blinding light.
It was such a personal and fundamental shift of viewpoint, and it

brought such freedom from old concerns and worries and such new satisfaction and effectiveness in daily existence, that it was called by the highest religious names, "realization," "eternal life," "the practice of the presence of God," "living in the Godhead," "I in God and God in me," and so on. It was something so startling and different that it had to be talked about, and passed on; and many a realizer made it a crusade to preach it to others—again as Galileo did with his new concepts of motion. These sudden shifts in perception-view cannot all be included in the "ecstasy" experiences that Marghanita Laski has collected, but some of them can. For example, the physicist Mach described in his own experience in this way:

> On a bright summer day in the open air, the world with my ego suddenly appeared to me as *one* coherent mass of sensations, only more strongly coherent in the ego. . . . This moment was decisive for my whole view.

This is one of the more subdued accounts.

The Mystical Formulations

I believe that when we understand the surprise and intensity of this sudden shift of perception, many of the odd phrases of even the religious mystics cease to be bizarre and ambiguous. They can be seen as fairly straightforward attempts to describe, sometimes with new language, these non-conventional aspects of the T-field which we have discussed; or attempts to make new and arresting phrases or analogies that would startle others into making the same jump of realization. (Once more, this is not so different from the attempts of Galileo and Newton and their successors to find a better terminology for motion.) If we identify the subjective with immediacy and directness and on-going participation in the world (like that of a decision-network), and with a complete and unique T-field which includes all objects but which is nowhere and cannot be pointed to, a T-field which is with us all the time but which is "outside of time" because it includes all time and has no birth and death and no self-world dichotomy—is not that the referential content of many of the mystical and oriental puzzle-phrases?

I think the idea of such a totality-field of perception and awareness is almost certainly a large part of what is meant by the "Thatness" or "Suchness" of Aldous Huxley in *The Perennial Philosophy*, and by the "Istigkeit" of Meister Eckhart, the "Vastness" or the "No-Thing" or "Nothing" of the Chinese philosophers, and the "divine Ground of Being" of the mystic saints. Yes, it is odd language;

but these men were intelligent and effective in their daily lives, they were not insane or stupid; should we not believe that they were trying to talk about something? The descriptions of the Way or the Tao sound very much like the properties of the total T-field, with special emphasis on immediacy, assurance, and straightforward action. "The Tao that can be named is not the Tao," says the Tao Te Ching, pointing to the language difficulty.

The loss of a distinguishable "self" in the one-ness of the subjective totality is often described by the mystics. Mach quotes Lichtenberg as writing, "We should say, *It thinks,* just as we say, *It lightens;*" and he adds, "The assumption, or postulation, of the ego is a mere practical necessity." Is this so different from what the interpreter of Zen, D. T. Suzuki, writes? He says:

> I am in Nature and Nature is in me. Not mere participation in each other, but a fundamental identity between the two. . . . The reason I can see the mountains as mountains and the waters as waters is because I am in them and they are in me; that is, *tat tvam asi* [Thou art That].

The German mystic, Meister Eckhart, was even more graphic about the unity. He said, "The eye with which I see God is the same eye with which God sees me," and he was nearly tried for heresy as a result.

The ego can either be said to have disappeared, or to include it all, which is the position many solipsists have started with. To quote Mach again, "The ego can be so extended as ultimately to embrace the entire world. (The virtuoso possesses as perfect a mastery of his instrument as he does of his own body.)"

This inclusiveness is the basis of some of Thomas Traherne's most beautiful passages. He says:

> You never enjoy the world aright till the sea itself floweth in your veins, till you are clothed with the heavens and crowned with the stars; and perceive yourself to be the sole heir of the whole world, and more than so, because men are in it who are every one sole heirs as well as you. . . .

And Traherne's description of his own shift of perception ends with the sense of encompassing everything:

> Something infinite behind everything appeared which talked with my expectations and moved my desire. The city seemed to stand in Eden, or to be built in Heaven. The streets were mine, the people were mine, their clothes and gold and silver were mine, as much as their sparkling eyes, fair skins and ruddy faces. The skies were mine,

and so were the sun and moon and stars, and all the world was mine; and I the only spectator and enjoyer of it.

The idea of the ongoing timeless moment which includes all time is in Thoreau, where he says, "That time which we really improve, or which is improvable, is neither past, present, nor future." This is the timeless "Moment" of Howard Nemerov's great poem, the moment when ". . . the mind of God, / the flash across the gap of being, thinks / in the instant absence of forever: now."

Many of these non-conventional perceptual properties of the T-field are summed up together in some of the verses that Suzuki quotes from the Third Patriarch of Zen:

When the deep mystery of one Suchness is fathomed,
All of a sudden we forget the external entanglements;
When the ten thousand things are viewed in their oneness,
We return to the origin and remain where we have always been. . . .
. . . . . .
When Mind and each believing mind are not divided,
and undivided are each believing mind and Mind,
This is where words fail,
For it is not of the past, present, or future.

What more is there to say about the totality-field of subjective perception?

The old texts also recognize that the "flip" to this view, the personal realization of the primacy and inclusiveness of the subjective, is not something that can be achieved by working for it. Like all the Gestalt-flips of perception, it is an all-or-none shift, not logically derivable from what has gone before (except perhaps as we have derived it here by a very roundabout method). It is something you may suddenly realize here and now, or at any moment, but it comes by insight as a "grace," and not as the result of any logic or effort. In Zen teaching, this sudden flip or perception-shift is the *satori* jump of enlightenment, the "Gateless Gate" through which the novice passes, as odd as a riddle and as close and startling as a blow. Or as Lawrence Durrell says, in *Clea:*

No amount of explanation can close the gap. Only realization! One day you are going to wake from your sleep shouting with laughter. *Ecco!*

Laughing, of course, at how simple it is, and how you have been fooled and led into unreal distractions and unending pursuits when the truly satisfying and eternal was *here,* all the time.

The Stages of Understanding

This jump to subjective realization is a most important jump. Yet by looking at our models, and ourselves, I think we can see a third and final stage of understanding that goes even beyond this perception-flip. Perhaps the best description of this last stage is given in another Zen saying from one of the old masters:

> When I began to study Zen, mountains were mountains;
> When I thought I understood Zen, mountains were no longer mountains;
> But when I came to full knowledge of Zen, mountains were again mountains.

It is a translation from another language and another century, but I think that in our present terms, it may mean something like the following. Before we have begun to think about the problem of perception and our relation to the external world, mountains and other objects are simply objects "out there," objects that we point to and talk about and think about in the ordinary objective way. But after we begin to examine the bases of perception, we realize that these mountains and objects we are seeing are not as simple as something "out there," but are our interpretations of distorted images on the retina, which are moved about in a complex way as we move ourselves or our eyeballs or manipulate the objects. So we realize that these "objects" are not merely objective but are subjective as well; they are "I-it" relationships, where the perception is personal and depends upon our participation, and has to be re-created or modified anew at every moment by our own actions.

But then, finally, I think we come to realize that this kind of analysis exists to be superseded, so to speak: that *these are the only mountains there are!* All our perceptions have this subjective aspect, and therefore it largely drops away in comparing one physical object with another. It is the non-subjective residues or invariances that differ between a mountain and a bump on a log, and these are what we cannot get rid of by wishing or rotating our eyeballs. It is these less subjective aspects that interest us and that are important for manipulation and survival. This is the way a decision-network organizes its world; this is what we mean by seeing mountains, and it is the only way we see mountains at all.

I think it is very dangerous for us to stop with the first of these stages, the objective stage, as we do throughout our society today. I know that the idea of one's world and oneself as being built up of objects has been the standard way of teaching in our atomizing and technological culture. Students, and professors and philosophers too, may grow up without ever being called to question it; in all our mechanisms it works so well! And this is undoubtedly the simplest way of teaching children quickly about structural relations and how to make and manipulate things, so as to lay the basis for technological accomplishment.

But by the time a child reaches adolescence, he should begin to be taught a juster picture of his personal relation to the world, as well. Such a restructuring could be of the greatest importance to us. For this almost universal objectivist view of ours is not only an inversion of the subjective perceptual basis of things, it is also, I think, a major source of the widespread feelings of dehumanization and meaninglessness and resentment in our national and world society.

Any error in our ideas of being will always lead to psychological and social pathology and dehumanization—whether it is a persecution complex, or the belief that all is predestined, or that all is subconscious, or that man lives for the state. The personal meaninglessness produced by the objectivist inversion of things is no exception. The healthiest change we could make today, scientifically and socially as well as theologically, would be to put back into the center the immediate and personal nature of awareness, responsibility, choice, and action; and to see that all our magnificent science and technology are derived from man, not man from science.

Yet it is also important not to stop at this second, subjective, stage either. Many who have made the jump to the subjective have ended by treating the objective as small and unimportant. Solipsist tyrants, believing that their will, like their eyeballs, could move mountains, have come to believe that it should trample over these small annoying figures in their visual field. There are many such, in jails and asylums, boasting and preaching that all is unreal and sometimes shooting to prove it. Others who have made the jump have been led instead to quietism and passivity. If the objective is unreal, all action is but striving; and this half-truth has simplified many men down to pure contemplation or begging, leaving it to other and more objective strivers to bring them the means of life.

Such over-subjectivism is as serious an error as over-objectivism. Perception stands on two legs, the subjective and the objective, and needs them both. We need to be not only human but whole; not only contemplators but doers. We need to go on to the third stage of understanding, to know not only the subjective, but through it to know the objective again. The objective is both primary, and derived; the subjective—on the other side of this invariant self-confirming loop that goes on and on—is both derived, and primary. When we reach this stage of understanding, we can see and act effectively on the objective "because it is the only objective there is," even while we appreciate the immediacy of the subjective and use it as our crucial continuing test of the reality and importance of the objective world we manipulate. Our planning and action and achievement can become satisfying and effective, because they are no longer tied to either the man-denying or the world-denying, because what we do is done with wholeness and realism, consonant at last with the way things are.

These stages in understanding perception are like the stages in understanding the staircase-figure, where we first make the Gestalt-jump from seeing the figure "from above" to seeing it "from below," but where finally, like the psychologist himself, we see the whole figure as containing both views, simultaneously a paradox and a unity.

Or they are like the stages we go through in understanding painting. To the very young child it may be only canvas and splashes of color, but as the child grows it becomes, it *is*, the representational world of funny or threatening figures. The teen-ager sees through all that; it is nothing but someone's daubs on cloth; he could do better. But then the adult, the connoisseur, finally comes to reacquire a sophisticated naïveté, an innocent eye again, so that he sees and appreciates it all—canvas and paint, figure and ground, technique and representation—and the whole constructive unity of the achievement, mind and matter, in all its aspects. This is the stage of the artist himself, the creative self-determining individual, who has passed through all the stages and can paint at last with both the mastery of the man and the seeing eye of the child. And in perception, I think that through the process of more complete understanding we may likewise reacquire the innocent eye, the confidence and curiosity of little children, and may reach again the sense of immediacy and the "awareness, spontaneity, and intimacy" that the therapist Eric Berne has emphasized.

A better understanding of perception is like the better understanding of our own vision that comes from knowing the optics of how our eyeballs work. From it, I think we can get a more satisfying and more effective understanding of who and what we are in the world, both subjectively and objectively, as surely as we get a better understanding of ourselves from using a mirror daily. A better understanding of perception could lead to a restructuring of our philosophical attitude in science with the emphasis changing from methodology or linguistic and semantic analysis toward the personal, to questions of curiosity and choice and conclusion. It could give us a new view of our subjective nature, supported by the fact that a number of features of the subjective human situation are strikingly like the properties of a decision-network viewed from within; and this could lead to an objective rediscovery of personal indeterminacy and freedom.

But the most important restructuring may be the correction of the common objectivist inversion that plagues and dehumanizes our whole technological society today. Many are beginning to feel that the primary reality of human existence cannot lie in any of our objective scientific results, in the atoms or explanations that we accept or reject, but must lie rather in the immediate realization of the here-and-now totality of awareness-and-action and human interaction, wherein scientific knowledge represents only a small and specialized subsection. As perception theory now suggests, each of us stands at the creative, choosing focus of a moving web of past antecedents and future consequences that branch out from our present choices and actions, propagating and amplifying themselves indefinitely. We interpenetrate the universe; it responds to our every breath. The proof is everywhere. We love each other, and the glance of our eyes begets new children. We teach, we learn; we organize and we respond; we plan and we achieve; we make the earth the creative center of the solar system. Great men and prophets have always known that they had this future-shaping seminal power. It is a creative fact that stands outside of physics; but we see that science may yet be reconciled.

When you get rid of the objectivist delusion, do you not feel the unitive focus, the creative power to act freely and differently in yourself, here, now? It is like a release from an obsession. It puts the focus back within. It gives us, as William James suggested, an immediacy, a sense of personal value and personal power, of awareness and action, that could reshape the world.

Our analysis here began with the riddle of the fish in the sea. But there is one version of the story in which the fish finally gets an answer. "Little fish, little fish, you live, move and have your being in the sea. The sea is within you and without you, and you are made of sea, and you will end in sea. The sea surrounds you as your own being."

I think that we, as decision-networks and human beings, as

thinking minds, are part of the sea of perception-and-action that reaches out and encompasses the universe. We began in sea and we will end in sea. The universe of awareness is the universe of action, and within it our two faces of perception, the subjective and the objective, are but the reversed emphases of a single reality, shaping each other. To see the world is to manipulate it. Every eyeblink, every turning of a page, every new bit of understanding, is an amplifying action that moves the world into a future continually re-created. And realization, the flip of perception, the awareness of this immediate and ongoing participation in the totality, is at our finger-tips, in the time between breathing out and breathing in.

III

The Limits of Reductionism

In the world's hierarchical complexity, higher levels depend on lower ones but develop new properties of their own.

"REDUCTIONISM" IS the philosophical belief that the more complex sciences can be reduced to simpler ones, at least in principle. Thus it implies that all of chemistry some day can be completely explained and predicted by a sophisticated application of the physics of atoms and electrons. In the same way, biology would some day be explainable by chemistry and physics, man and his brain would some day be explainable by the operation of his biological components, and social interactions and problems would be explainable by the behavior of individual men.

This philosophy has had powerful successes, and for several hundred years our thinkers have had the continual expectation that if we just keep working we will always find that complex problems can be reduced to simpler ones, so that this seems plausible and obvious to most scientists and most philosophers of science. Nevertheless, there are a number of aspects of our study and analysis of the complex external world that limit the application of reductionism, even in principle. These limitations grow out of the following considerations:

—*Different approximations* are needed and are generated in different domains of science, with unimportant correction terms in one domain—like gravity in the field of nuclear physics—becoming dominant features in another.

—Each science is *open-ended*—still developing—at any given time, so any attempt to make from it a closed derivation of another science is always incomplete, with the chance that this opens up of the derivation being wrong.

—A science exhaustive in its own domain may still miss completely some other *aspect* of the problem—as the exhaustive physics and

74

chemistry of a neon sign may still miss the fact that it spells "Joe's Bar and Grill" in English.

—In systems of *hierarchical complexity,* the higher levels of organization must be consistent with the lower ones but are not necessarily predictable from them, any more than a "systems phenomenon" like a traffic jam—or the absence of one—is predictable from a complete knowledge of the physics and chemistry of an individual automobile and its driver.

—There is a difference between *explaining* a developed subject in terms of a simpler one—for example, my detailed path on an auto trip to Chicago, in terms of the physics of the wheels and the bumps in the road and the guidance system—and *being able to predict* the former in terms of the latter.

—Both reductionism and antireductionism are *non-disprovable* because of the open-ended character of science, which may turn up new confirmations or exceptions at any future time. This means that reductionism, or its opposite, cannot be a scientific theory or proof, but is more like a heuristic *program,* or an attitude, or a statement of faith. In fact, both attitudes are needed in a healthy science, the one as a pressure to make our views of the world mutually consistent, the other as a stimulus to new insights or new paradigms that can turn upside down the received science of a given time, and permit growth.

An examination of these limitations from the point of view of the hierarchical complexities of science throws more light on several of them.

Hierarchical organization and systems properties. The importance of the notion of hierarchical systems can be seen if we consider the full scale of the sizes of things. For example, let us start at the level of atoms and molecules and macromolecules and go up to cells, organisms, and societies. The molecular level ranges from systems with the dimensions of 1 atom, up to molecules and macromolecules with 10^3 and 10^6 atoms. In the case of cells we get up to possibly 10^{15} atoms, in the case of organisms to something like 10^{29}, and in the case of societies to 10^{38}, giving a quasi-logarithmic scale very roughly but typically like the following (the ranges of sizes in each category are not shown):

1	10^3	10^6	10^{15}	10^{29}	10^{38}
atom	molecule	macromolecule	cell	organism	society

The first thing to emphasize about this scale is that the difference between the big systems and the small ones is not just a "similarity transformation." Going from small sizes to big sizes in the case of organized systems requires an *addition of information*. The situation is accordingly quite different, say, from the enlargement of a crystal, which represents no more than a trivial increase of information, if any, because of the physical similarity between the large crystal and the small one. In biological systems, if we go from a short segment of a hereditary chain of DNA to a large, long segment of DNA, it appears that there is a roughly linear increase of information (except for some unknown redundancies of segments). And this is recoverable, *operational* information, because the effects of each individual base pair at each point of the chains can be amplified up to macroscopic and observable effects, such as the presence of a blood disease in an animal or human being. The differences in the levels of information as we go from the largest protein molecules up to single-celled animals, or from these animals up to large organisms, or from organisms up to cultural societies, are factors of thousands or millions or more at each step.

This means that we are dealing with hierarchical organizations which develop systems properties that go far beyond the properties of the subsystems. I think it is very doubtful whether they are even in principle predictable from the properties of the subsystems. Take the example of a traffic jam, which is a phenomenon occurring at the level of social interaction. The possibility of a traffic jam is a systems-property of all the cars in a certain region of the country. It is not predictable from the physics and chemistry of the explosion of gasoline in the cylinders or the design of the steering systems of the automobiles. The jam is generated, or is resolved, at the systems level, not at the automobile level. If you have a low density of cars in the county, you do not get the traffic jam, while if you have a high density of cars, you do—regardless of driver behavior or specific accidents of individual cars.

You may choose to regard the traffic-jam systems behavior as "reducible" to the subsystems behavior, or you may not, but the jam is certainly describable more easily in terms of the higher-level systems-properties rather than in terms of the multiple-detailed individual complexities of the subsystem interactions, most of which are irrelevant to the final general result. Certainly the systems-properties at the higher level of the hierarchy are not easily predictable from the properties of the sub-systems at the lower level. It is true that a sufficiently detailed and insightful application of computers over a long period of time might permit the extraction of general properties, like traffic jams, invariant to the detailed subsystem interactions. But such a procedure begs the question of how we decide which of an infinity of derivable general properties the computer is to search for. And, in addition, there are many, many hierarchical systems where it is simply not practical in a finite lifetime, with a finite computer capacity, to jump across several levels—5 or 10 or 15 orders of magnitude—of a hierarchical organization in a predictive way. In such cases, reductionism might be abstractly tenable, but the daily operations of science in real time have to proceed by a different route, by studying each level of the hierarchy in terms of its own regularities of organization and not in terms of those at some other level.

The different aspects of a system. The difficulty in making predictions from one level of organization to another is a special case of a more general point—that a complete and exhaustive description of one aspect of a system may in fact be carried out without any mention of some other aspect of the system. Thus, in the case of the neon sign, as Donald Mackay has emphasized, one might know all about the physics and engineering, the electrical behavior of the individual atoms and ions in the gas discharge tube, the construction and properties of the electrodes and the glass tube, and the electrical connections to the transformers and the city generators— and still not know that the sign says "Joe's Bar and Grill" in English. The message on the sign is a linguistic and social and historical aspect which has no place in the time-invariant physics of the problem. What has "meaning" at the social level of interaction is generally quite "meaningless" at the different level of examination of the detailed motion of the atoms and molecules.

Different approximations in different domains. The hierarchical scale also brings us up against the general fact that the laws of science valid in any domain are only approximations with a certain range of validity, and that they change in going to a different range of size or domain of inquiry. For example, in dealing with the hydrogen atom, the most accurate equation at present is the Dirac equation. Even this elegant equation is not correct; for 20 years we have known that it must be patched up with an important little Band-Aid called the polarization of the vacuum (and who knows what smaller Band-Aids must eventually be added on top of this one?) Even so, no one can solve the Dirac equation for larger atoms than the hydrogen atom, or at least no one has succeeded in doing so. The result is that we approximate larger systems by using the simpler Schrödinger equation. But no one can solve the Schrödinger equation with its relativistic components for more than a three-particle system, and so we go on to the still more approximate Hartree-Fock equation. But the Hartree-Fock equation in its turn becomes so complex that one can hardly extend it to even as heavy an atom as copper. To make an accurate *a priori* calculation of the differences between the properties of copper and nickel—which only differ by one electron, but whose differences are obvious to any man with coins in his hand!—would be almost unthinkable as a practical computer-program today if we were to base it on the fundamental Dirac or Schrödinger equations including relativistic corrections.

This example, entirely within the supposedly fundamental domain of atomic physics itself, is only a special case of the general rule that approximations that are valid at one level are no longer valid at another. In the little puddle in the street, the ripples are dominated by surface tension, while in the Pacific Ocean the waves are dominated by gravity. As you go from the one scale to the other, the surface tension becomes relatively insignificant. In the hydrogen atom the relativity correction to the energy is about 10^{-5} of the total energy, but the correction increases as the fourth power of the atomic number, so that this meaningless, trivial, negligible correction in computing chemical reaction or binding energy for the little hydrogen atom becomes a correction of hundreds of electron-volts in the iron atom. At the present time, no physicist or chemist has actually been able to demonstrate that these hundreds of volts do not have modifications that affect binding, in iron or the heavier atoms. How then do you expect to predict, by quantum mechanics, the behavior of the iron-porphyrin molecules, or the iron cytochromes, or hemoglobin? If we still, after forty years of quantum mechanics, cannot cross reliably this simple gap of a little more than one order of magnitude in electron number, when would the reductionist expect this gap, or any larger gap, to be closed? As long as chemical binding cannot be computed from quantum mechanics with certainty, it evidently has to be measured first by experimental chemists, who can then tell the quantum theorist, with nonreductionist direct evidence, whether his calculations have put in enough corrections accurately or not.

Perhaps the most dramatic example of this kind that we know occurs in the case of gravity. The physicists who look at atoms and molecules would probably never have predicted the existence of gravity if they had always been limited in their observations to the atomic world. The reason is that gravity is only about 10^{-39} times the size of the strong electrical interactions in atoms. At the present time, even with lasers, we are only beginning to reach accuracies of 10^{-12} to 10^{-15} in our most exact measurements. It would be hopeless to measure or to check any theory of correction terms at the 10^{-39} level, unless fantastic cancellation occurred in some phenomenon, or unless these terms became important in some other range where they could be studied independently rather than derivatively. How then can gravity be so important to us large bodies when it is so trivial at the atomic level? It is because there *is* a fantastic cancellation: the interactions that were absolutely dominant down at the atomic level all cancel out when we have 10^{30} or 10^{40} atoms, leaving behind that absolutely negligible residue of gravity which did not cancel out and which thus becomes the most important phenomenon at the planetary level. The possibility of predicting or extrapolating these trivial corrections correctly from one domain to another is something which has yet to be demonstrated.

Open-endedness of each science. This limited domain of approximations means that every science is subject to additional unforeseen corrections as it extends its domain, and is therefore inherently open-ended. At any given instant in physics and chemistry —if these are ongoing subjects in which our understanding of the trivial corrections is not yet complete—any attempt to reduce some higher-order subject to these supposedly more basic subjects is likely to be upset by some amplification of the most negligible of corrections not yet observed or computed. We see that any thoroughgoing reductionism therefore amounts to an assertion that the more basic subject is now known to be completely closed down to its last corrections, a thing that no scientists and few philosophers would ever want to admit for any field. A science which is continually developing, in which there are still some things left for our children to discover, must be perpetually incomplete, or at least of some degree of uncertainty as to its completeness. This is the most fundamental obstacle, as I see it, to any real-time assertion of reductionism. A thoroughgoing reductionism which, by the nature of science itself, can never be explicitly demonstrated at any given epoch, thus becomes a problem in infinite regress, a will-o'-the-wisp that should be as unsatisfactory to operationally minded philosophers as it is useless to science itself.

It seems to me, therefore, that reductionism is not something that can be proved, but that it is rather, as Everett Mendelsohn has emphasized, a *program*—or perhaps something more like an attitude, or an article of scientific faith. It is undoubtedly a magnificent program, always pressing toward the unity of science; and it is a program full of continually fruitful suggestions as it looks for regularities across the borders, and one to which all scientists must in large degree subscribe. But it is a program that will never be completed, at least not until we have believed for perhaps 40 or 100 or 2000 years that physics and chemistry are complete, with nothing more to be said about them even at the 10^{-39} level, and until we believe that our computers are able to compute all the extrapolations and systems-properties to other domains and other levels of the hierarchy with sufficient accuracy to make experiments in other fields unnecessary. Until that time, every field must continue to do its own experimentation and discover its own approximations, and continue to create and manipulate its own symbols and regularities, and then simply raise the question whether these are consistent with the lower-level approximations that are known at the time.

This leads to even longer thoughts. Who can say, for example, that there is not some further correction at the 10^{-78} level which only becomes significant and measurable at galactic distances? We see that ultimately there may be no "lower level" of more basic science. Each domain must inform all the others, the complex the simple, and the large the small. This is not reductionism, but interactionism.

It will give us more perspective if we remind ourselves that in every era some great discoveries have been essentially unanticipated from the physics and chemistry of the time. Remember that it was the biologists who discovered current electricity. The physicists might not have discovered it for a hundred years, for they were looking at stars. It was biologists who discovered that bats avoid obstacles in the dark; the more sober and fundamental scientists said this was wishful thinking or vitalism, or some such dirty word, and then later found the echo-ranging mechanism. It was biologists and geologists who said that geological-times must have extended backwards for millions of years, and Kelvin said, "That's absurd; why don't you people be scientific? We can prove that the sun cannot have lasted that long." And it couldn't, according to his mechanism of solar energy generation. But it wasn't the sun's lifetime that was limited, it was Kelvin's imagination.

I think we must insist on the right and necessity of each of our fields of science to organize its own observations, and then and only then to see how far they can be interpreted in terms of lower levels of organization. A field must not reject its own real regularities if they do not fit those from other supposedly more fundamental fields. Such situations should be carefully scrutinized for error, of course; but if the new regularities are indeed based on well-made observations and sound statistics, they may be simply the first signs of a new scientific revolution, as has happened so often in the past.

Non-disprovability of reductionism or anti-reductionism. But if reductionism is not provable—or disprovable—in real time, then by the same token antireductionism is not provable or disprovable. Are not these different absolutist claims the result of different personal attitudes that often come simply from differences of temperament? It seems to me that both kinds of attitude or temperament are needed in a healthy science. At a given moment of history it is important for some men to say, "Oh, we can surely explain these regularities in terms of simpler subsystems." But it is also important for other men to say, "Your simple subsystem approach is sterile; its ideas are incomplete and its predictions dubious when so extended; we cannot know, without checking, how far they will extend into other domains; we must keep on the lookout for new principles coming to the fore." How can we continue to have new approaches in complex fields unless we have some men who believe that the phenomena are not adequately covered by supposedly more basic explanations?

This dialogue must continue as long as science continues. If men should ever accept a conclusive victory by one side or the other, the dialogue would stop, and science would be dead. It seems to me, therefore, that the reductionists and the antireductionists, like the deductive and the inductive types of mind, both have a permanent role to play. Science is a balance of opposites in the search for new regularities. The believers in regularity must not discourage the searchers for the new, while the searchers for the new in their turn must not disparage the on-going search for further reduction, if science is to continue to be a living venture.

IV

Beauty, Pattern and Change

*We continually search for patterns, but patterns that contain the
unexpected.*

Poetry is a superior amusement: I do not mean an amusement for
superior people . . . If we think of the nature of amusement, then poetry is not amusing; but if we think of anything else that poetry may
seem to be, we are led into far greater difficulties . . . [Other classic
definitions of poetry are] frigid to anyone who has felt the full surprise and elevation of a new experience of poetry.

THIS CRYPTIC AESTHETIC COMPARISON is from T. S. Eliot's preface to
the 1928 edition of *The Sacred Wood*. It is at first sight a puzzling
statement, and those who regard Eliot's poetry as an obscure joke—
an amusement!—may think this is cut from the same cloth. But I
want to take it here as a kind of text whose meaning will become
clearer as we examine the nature and evolution of perception, the
role of change-in-stimulation for every complex stimulus-response
system or organism, and its newly discovered relation to such peculiarly human responses as amusement and aesthetic appreciation in
the highly developed human organism. I hope to show that Eliot's
statement, even from a scientific and psychological point of view, is
a serious and important insight, and that when we do think about
the nature of amusement and surprise as indicated by various studies today, the statement ceases to be cryptic and becomes natural
and even obvious, and can be applied not only to verbal arts like
poetry but also to the musical arts and the arts of design.

Actually only a part of the aesthetic problem of art will concern us here, but it is the most curious and difficult part. Most critics agree that art has two aspects, a formal aspect and a representational aspect. It is easy to see why we may be pleased and satisfied
by the representational elements in art—by the moment of prayer
in "The Angelus" or the thunderstorm in the Pastoral Symphony.

They resemble our own moments of heightened experience. It is not so easy to see why a full-grown and intelligent adult is deeply satisfied by the formal elements in art. That is, by space and time patterns and the deviations from them, as in the development of the theme in a quartet or in the balancing of the painting by a touch of red in the opposite corner. This problem of formal beauty is the one to which Eliot and the other formal theorists have addressed themselves.

This problem has recently begun to yield to analytical examination from two sides: first from the side of aesthetic analysis, particularly in the field of musical aesthetics, assisted by some general ideas from "information theory"; second from the side of the physics of perception. It now appears that the requirements for aesthetic enjoyment are simply the requirements for perception itself, raised to a higher degree; and the essential thing in each case is to have *a pattern that contains the unexpected*. This seems to be the heart of what we call beautiful, and it is no exaggeration to say that men need it as they need food.

I hope to justify this view here not by means of rigorous deductions from accepted premises nor by experimental proofs, but rather by a sort of ramble through a number of fields, from natural science on the one hand to aesthetic criticism on the other. To outline the argument briefly, I want to show that the mind's grasp and enjoyment of the external world rest on two complementary neuropsychological principles: the principle of response to novelty or change-in-stimulation, and the principle of response to repetition or pattern. We will begin by noting that response to changes-in-stimulation, and specific and patterned changes at that, is fundamental to life and goes back to the beginnings of organic evolution and even before. Moreover, the physiology and structure of the brain suggest that its function is to select patterns for response out of a tremendous flux of information inputs. We will go on to the recent archaeological evidence, which demonstrates that the human brain has evolved almost explosively under the stresses of the post-glacial world so as to cope selectively with patterns of the highest complexity.

We will then turn to the psychophysical evidence on the role of pattern in the brain's organization of external experience, as given by current ideas on visual perception or "how we see straight lines"; in vision at least, the experimental evidence seems to confirm the theoretical conclusion that neither a steady flux nor an unpatterned random flux can be organized into experience. Taken all together, this evidence from different fields for the central role played by pattern and by change-of-pattern in the functioning of a central organ such as the brain strongly suggests that these features of the input flux may have an affective as well as an informational significance, not only in the representation of external objects but as pattern *qua* pattern; and in fact that the affective and the informational aspects of response to pattern may be indissoluble.

This conclusion seems to be confirmed by examining what critics have said about the role of patterns or symmetries in the visual arts, where the symmetries can play simultaneously not only a formal role but also a representational role because of the presence and "naturalness" of symmetric patterns in the biological world. Finally our ramble will turn to the role of pattern-expectations, and of surprise and randomness and the unexpected, and their humorous or pleasurable affect, in current aesthetic theories of music and the other arts; and this will being us back again with renewed understanding to the poetic problem we have posed here at the beginning.

In these times of defiant analysis or defiant opposition to analysis in the humanities, a word of justification may be needed for this kind of wandering back and forth among the analytical sciences, psychology, and poetry. The justification lies in the fact that the study of patterns and how the brain responds to them is necessarily an interdisciplinary subject. Anyone interested in a full account of the peculiarities and powers of the human brain must be prepared to discuss it in several languages. We see the brain at various times from the inside or from the outside, emotionally or historically or by dissection, as a piece of watery tissue, or as a weapons system, or as the creator of philosophy. All the disciplines are needed, and evidence from several different ones will be introduced here. With such an approach, there is a danger of being found superficial by specialists; but in searching for the central elements in so extensive a problem, it is not as important at first to go deep into the different kinds of description as it is to be sure that they are mutually consistent and that the general picture is complete.

What is particularly likely to offend many persons is an apparent "reduction" of humanistic appreciation to mere mathematics and biology. It smacks not only of pedantry, which we always excuse, but of dissection, which we do not. It looks like the work of a calculating and joyless mind, one that would pull the wings off a bird in order to analyze flight. But I think an unwillingness to converse in both types of language is part of the breakdown in communications between the humanities and the sciences that C. P. Snow discussed in *The Two Cultures and the Scientific Revolution.*

The truth is that we need both types of language, and easy translations between them. The situation is like the problem of whether to discuss the physiological basis of love. For the intelligent mind, love is not belittled but enlarged by physiological understanding. This is what guarantees that the emotion is a yes-saying of the whole organism and not just a disembodied sentimentality. Likewise with the appreciation of beauty: In music or art or poetry, an understanding of the physiological and physical basis of our aesthetic response is what can guarantee that it is consistent with civilized intelligence and judgment and is not merely a rationalized jungle dance. If someone says it is absurd to drag in the language of evolution and science to discuss the poetic experience, I reply, Who told you to compartmentalize? The human mind is *one;* it is absurd not to.

THE PRIMITIVENESS OF RESPONSE
TO STIMULI

Let us begin our ramble toward the aesthetic problem by bringing out a number of paradoxes about the physics and physiology and evolution of perception. One paradox is that our response system demands new information or novelty, and yet at the same time demands regularity or pattern. A second paradox is that these properties of the response system are both very old in their evolutionary origins and yet very new in their recent and sudden elaboration in the human brain.

In higher animals, the nervous system is a device for responding with great discrimination to the environment. Its response involves a selective double amplification system. For example, in the visual process, the light images carrying information from the environment strike the rods and cones of the retina and are amplified first into electrical-chemical nerve pulses that travel back along the neurons. At any instant, there are about 100 million of these input pulses passing into the processing centers of the retina and the brain. What happens to them then is still obscure, but somehow all the visual and nonvisual inputs become collated into either a memory or a new "decision," a kind of self-consistent order to the oculomotor and other muscles, about every twentieth of a second. Each decision may be proliferated into millions of motor impulses which are then amplified a second time as the individual muscles make the ordered response to the changing environmental situation. It is a beautiful thing to watch such a system operating at maximum capacity. The most complex continuous performance in the whole animal kingdom may be that of a skilled pianist sight-reading Bach.

It is obvious that such a sophisticated type of response did not develop out of nothing. Its roots must go back, at least in some form, to the very beginnings of organic evolution. A little consideration shows that the response to stimulation and the demand for information from the environment must have been coeval with life itself. Before there were networks of neurons, before there were single neurons, there was selective response. At a sufficiently early stage, in fact, there was probably no distinction between nervous and muscular response, or between chemical and electrical transmission of signals. In an ionic medium such as the living cell, every chemical signal has an electrical component, and vice versa. Muscle and nerve cells are alike in many of their electrical and contractile properties, and at the level of flatworms they are even said to stain alike. The flatworm probably does not care whether his signal is propagated by a twitch or a pulse, so long as it is adequate.

And even within a single-cell organism there can be a network of communications fibrils, as biologists know from the delicate neuromotor fibrillar network inside a *Paramecium*. (Such micronetworks within a cell might also be important in higher brains.) Still lower down the scale, in precellular systems, there must have been some elementary kind of response organization. In fact, the simplest imaginable self-reproduction, whatever the chemical types of the molecules involved, requires the acquisition by the reproducing system of suitable "food" molecules and no others, and so must show some selectivity of response. When the molecules in the solution around such a growing and self-reproducing system are of the wrong kind or touch it at the wrong place or time, nothing happens. But when the right molecule touches the system at the right place, presto! There is a release of chemical energy, and a new bond is formed, carrying the system one step farther toward completed reproduction. This is a selected amplification of the input contact "stimulus" into a "response." At this level the specification of such a response is usually regarded as being in the province of chemistry or biochemistry, but it would be meaningless to debate whether it is primarily a change of chemical structure or of mechanical shape or of electrical charge. All these aspects will be involved in the elementary act.

And I would say that this kind of chemical selectivity and amplification and response even enters into the still earlier selective chemistry of "inorganic evolution," from which we believe the first living or self-duplicating molecules were built up. We pride ourselves on our own mental abilities in manipulating the environment. But any selective response to a stimulus does the same. Mind developed out of selective response; and selective response goes all the way back to the origin of life and, quite possibly, even before.

STRUCTURE AND FUNCTION OF THE BRAIN

Let us consider next the gross structure and physiology of our brains, a subject as important to our discussion as their pre-Adamite ancestry. The brain makes up only about 2 percent of our body weight, but is now provided with about 20 percent of the resting oxygen consumption and blood supply. It is the organ most sensitive to oxygen deficiency. Even if we knew nothing about what the brain does, this oxygen demand would prove that it is an organ designed for complete and rapid processing of something.

I think there is no doubt about what it is processing. It is input information. The flow and volume of the signals are so prodigious that one can easily see why they add up to this great physiological demand for blood and oxygen. With those 10^8 visual inputs or perhaps 10^9 inputs of all kinds fresh every millisecond, and those 20 decisions to be made every second, the brain consumes information as a stomach consumes food, only more continuously and with more imperious demands both for fresh information and for the energy needed to process it.

What is demanded is not merely information-signals but variations in the signals, as has been shown experimentally quite conclusively in the case of visual perception. As we noted earlier, it has recently been found that "scanning"—motion of the eyeball over the visual field—is necessary in order to have any sensation of vision at all. Riggs, Ditchburn, and their co-workers measured the motions of the eyeball by a photoelectric detector, and found that when a person is trying to fixate a point of light, his eyeball is oscillating all the time through a range of about one half minute of arc and at a frequency of the order of 100 cycles per second. This motion is of course too delicate and rapid to be detected visually by the visual process which it mediates. The eyeball not only trembles in this way, but it also changes direction suddenly from time to time and drifts, somewhat more slowly, so that the image wanders about continually over the fovea.

Both groups of workers compensated these motions of the eyeball by using electronic-optical feedback devices and corneal lens devices to form a "stabilized image" on the retina. This was when they made their odd discovery that, as soon as such a stabilization begins, vision ceases within a fraction of a second. The edges of patterns appear to blur out and the perceptual field becomes a uniform gray. The subject has a sensation of stress, and his eyeball makes wilder and wilder excursions. It is said to be a great relief if the eyes overshoot the stabilization limits of the apparatus so that vision reappears for a second. (Perhaps the origin of this relief is similar to that of the relief produced in other stimulus-deprivation experiments when the deprivation ends.)

What this dependence of vision on movement means is that our perceptual system is not equipped to detect really steady inputs, but only fluctuating inputs, and that its own motions are normally used to produce these fluctuations. Such "reafferent stimulation" or "stimulation that changes as a consequence of movements of the recipient organism" may always play a vital role in perception, as Held and others have emphasized. It may be that perception without participation is impossible.

The result is that as we noted earlier, the visual system is not a d.c. or "direct-current" detecting system, but an a.c. or "alternating" system. Sharpness of boundaries is an important factor in maximizing the alternations or fluctuations of input, and the automatic focusing mechanism of the eye is operating all the time to make the image boundaries as sharp as possible. The sharp or the highly contrasting object draws our immediate attention, and we follow it, perhaps because it offers us sharper fluctuations. The now-famous two-color illusions of Edwin Land depend critically upon sharpness of focus, which may be evidence that fluctuations play an important role in color perception also.

Conceivably fluctuation is as necessary for hearing as for vision. It is true that in a steady tone, the sound pulses always represent a pulsating physical stimulus (just as in a steady light the single photons represent a pulsating physical stimulus), but lower-frequency variations of pitch or intensity are probably necessary for effective stimulation. We cease to notice a continued steady tone, and warbling notes are used for warning. It is said that even persons with absolute pitch have difficulty in identifying the pitch of a perfectly pure sine wave input.

Therefore, if we say that the brain consumes and demands information, we are not using these words lightly. The nervous system oscillates for information, that is, for the variable, the contrasting, and the least expected; it tracks it down; and if none is to be had, perhaps it invents it, as Held has suggested. I think this is the simplest way to summarize the meaning of curiosity and attention and boredom, and of the aberrations and hallucinations of stimulus-deprivation experiments (when a human being wears a blindfold and ear plugs and lies in a soft bed or warm bath so that he is cut off from any stimuli for a day or more). And now I am no longer using the word "information" to mean merely stimuli or light images from the external world. I am using it in the full technical sense of information theory, a sense which Warren Weaver has explained very well in discussing the mathematical theory of communication:

> Information is . . . a measure of one's freedom of choice in selecting a message. The greater this freedom of choice, and hence the greater the information, the greater is the uncertainty that the message actually is some particular one. Thus greater freedom of choice, greater uncertainty, greater information go hand in hand.

The mind seeks to escape from the certainties of the diffuse light that remains during stimulus-deprivation. It is bored by the certainties of any humdrum job or routine entertainment. It seeks out the single moving spot on the landscape or the tiny squeak in the engine. It plays the slot machine to exhaustion, hoping for the rare and unpredictable payoff when the three lemons turn up. What it seeks in the variable light signals, and what it processes and responds to on all levels, is information—the changing, the novel, the surprising, and the uncertain.

Nevertheless, having emphasized this need for novelty, we must turn around and consider the other branch of our first paradox, namely, the need for regularity or pattern in our input information. The mind demands pattern, and it is easy to show that this must also be a primitive and essential need. For consider what kind of connections are required to make a response network efficient. A human being has of the order of 10^9 input channels from all his senses. He may have a similar number of output channels, or possibly somewhat fewer. It would obviously be fruitless to have each input matched up with only one output, like a billion reflex arcs laid side by side; because with a billion different inputs at each instant, we should then have a billion uncoordinated and conflicting outputs also. It follows that if we are to have a unique and self-consistent set of outputs without internal conflict between them, cross-connections are necessary between these arcs; and extensive ones, too, so that essentially every input signal can be collated with every other one before the unitary output decision is made.

But cross-connections mean that the response is not to any single input alone, but to the whole array or pattern of inputs. A single input would give only one alternative, on or off, and only one output behavior, on or off; making the other inputs unnecessary. It is therefore a fundamental axiom that any many-element receptor system, any organism with more than one sensory input spot (even *Paramecium!*) is necessarily a pattern-selecting or pattern-perceiving system. Pattern perception must be almost as primordial as response itself, and must have a role that has grown to vast importance in a brain with 10^9 inputs.

It is an amusing exercise to try to schematize our many-channel input-output system by drawing on a sheet of paper a dozen parallel input-output lines (since 10^9 is too many to draw). If we then try to add to these lines a distinguishable set of cross-connections, and cross-connections of the cross-connections between and around them, we can see immediately how the three-dimensional physical pattern would almost necessarily swell into a "great raveled knot," which is what the brain has been called. Possibly the convolutions of the brain have just this kind of physical necessity, as being a physically efficient way of packing an indefinitely growing number of cross-connections; just as the quite differently shaped convolutions of the intestines have a kind of physical necessity, in providing a large surface-to-volume ratio for a continuous tube in a small space. If this is so, the shape of the convolutions of the brain is a sort of visible proof of cross-connections and therefore of a mode of operation based on pattern perception.

RECENCY OF EVOLUTION
OF THE BRAIN

And now, having emphasized the antiquity of the nervous response to stimuli and to pattern, we must also turn around to the other branch of the second paradox and emphasize exactly the opposite, namely, the astonishingly recent evolution of the highly developed brains that we have. The anthropological evidence of Washburn and Howells and Leakey and others shows that our brains have roughly tripled in size since the discovery of fire and tools and speech. Our thumbs seem to have moved around to the opposed position in the same period. The internal and external changes occurred together, and apparently we have a newly developed tool-using brain to operate the new tool-using thumb.

The current view is that this development of the brain may have occurred in roughly two million years. On an evolutionary time scale, this is an absolutely explosive development of a new species or a new capacity. Our brains and our powers have enlarged with spectacular rapidity, and there is no reason to suppose that they are not still enlarging at the same rate!

There must have been a reason for this enlargement, a challenge which brought it forth. The anthropological evidence shows what it was, and what kinds of situations these brains were evolved to cope with. The external problem for pre-man and early man was the problem of coming out of the trees into a new environment and of manipulating tools, fire, and speech so as to survive during the ice ages. It appears from geological evidence that ice ages were essentially unprecedented within the experience of mammals. So were tools and fire. One suspects that upon this daring species of primates—using tools and weapons and fire not only against the cold and the other animals but against each other—novel situations of all kinds may have crowded in at a rate faster than any species had ever experienced before and survived. In every generation, in every year, and sometimes every day, they had to search over and over again for the crucial regularities in the flux of strangeness. It was learn or die. What our brain was evolved to deal with was continuous novelty of pattern. It should therefore be no surprise to find that that is what it is prepared to deal with and demands to deal with today.

FUNCTIONAL GEOMETRY
AND THE NECESSARY
SYMMETRIES OF PERCEPTION

The second phase of my argument comes closer to the actual aesthetic problem. It deals with the basic role of patterns in our visual perception. Certain problems of perception are peculiar to big brains with vast numbers of sensory elements. A beginning has been made on these problems, and some of the results can be summarized here.

Consider what it means to have the enormous number of 10^8 elements packed into a biological mosaic receptor such as the human retina. Since this is a piece of tissue which has been subject to all the accidents and irregularities of biological growth, and since the arrangement of the receptor cells looks random under the microscope—very different from the orderly arrangement in the little insect eye—it seems almost a certainty that this great number of elements could not have been individually prelocated, say on the basis of genetic information, with any great precision. It is then hard to see how the brain can "know where the cells are" or can make any visual discriminations that depend on their precise location. If the cells have a microscopic uncertainty of location, one would suppose that a line appearing straight to one man would appear full of little wiggles to his twin brother; the amplitude of the wiggles would indicate the limits of accuracy of the genetic specification.

Yet our actual discrimination and precision in certain visual observations is fantastic. The trouble may be, as we discussed earlier, that we are looking at the problem in the wrong way in emphasizing the precision of location of individual cells. But the new method of "functional geometry," which involves moving the eye over a field and comparing the signals received at one time with those received at another, permits us to make accurate discriminations without having to know exactly where the individual sensory elements are located.

To repeat what was said earlier, the method works as follows. Consider the array of light signals from all the rods and cones. (By "array," I mean a set of signals with no specified relationships between them; by "pattern," a set containing some relationship.) If this array is the same after some particular rotation of the eyeball —if the array is then "congruent" to an earlier array—this means there is some pattern, something in the external field which is congruent to itself after such a displacement of the array, resulting from the rotation. The brain can then perceive such a something if it can only detect the "sameness" of the array before and after the displacement—which is about the weakest requirement one could impose on a network. And the perception can be made without "knowing" where any of the receptor cells are individually located.

A straight line is such a self-congruent something, since it is congruent to itself and the array remains unchanged under any displacement along it. The array of signals from parallel lines would also be self-congruent under any displacement along the lines. Note that the images on the retina or on the cortex can be as crooked as you please without destroying the self-congruence, since all that is required is that the image fall on the same locus after displacement, and it makes no difference what that locus is. The discrimination is for straightness or parallelism in the *external* field. A circle is also self-congruent, but under rotations—which the eye can in fact perform. Concentric circles are likewise. Equidistant repeated patterns —"periodic" patterns—are self-congruent for unit displacements (discrete translations) in the direction of the repetition.

Congruence is also possible in the time dimension. Any space or sound array which is repeated after an interval or is repeated periodically is self-congruent in time. Audition may also have its own "stationary" self-congruent patterns similar to those of vision. One can imagine that octave or harmonic relationships between tones involve congruent excitation patterns on the basilar membrane of the ear. (It would be interesting to know whether changes of tension in this membrane could be used for "scanning" the excitation patterns.)

One advantage of the self-congruent method of perceiving patterns is that it is invariant to damage or loss of the receptor cells, or to blind spots. This method therefore makes it easier to understand psychological "closure" and also the extrapolation of patterns, which on a deeper level is called induction.

For the experienced adult eye, it might not be necessary to scan every new straight line afresh to determine its approximate straightness. Certain retinal elements may have been associated so often in past straight-line perceptions that when these elements are excited again and give off the same chorus of signals, we are satisfied of the straightness of the new object without further scanning. A single high-speed flash of light permits an adult to read all the writing in his 1-degree foveal circle; so retinal elements may be associated in letter relationships as well as straight-line relationships. After learning many such association patterns, the brain knows all it needs to know about the location of the individual receptors (although it might forget under retinal damage or stimulus deprivation).

Nevertheless this method of pattern perception would require that an infant or a visually naive adult (after removal of a congenital cataract, for example) might require long scanning and study to determine the straightness of a line; and this is in fact the case. This is consistent with D. O. Hebb's doctrine that perceptual organization even of such apparently primitive relationships as straightness or triangularity is only acquired—learned—through visual experience.

Arthropods can learn almost nothing, and birds can learn only certain things. It follows that much if not all of their pattern-perceiving system is prelocated and preconnected, from genetic information alone. This involves a great limitation on an individual animal's responses and powers in the presence of any situation completely new to his species. To escape this limitation it is necessary to develop a new type of pattern perception, one capable of jumping conceptual gaps and of learning, perhaps by using methods such as functional geometry that permit the learning of regularities that go beyond the genetic information. Such an escape is obviously needed for a really big brain with a billion inputs. These considerations add weight to our earlier anthropological conclusion that pattern learning may be the faculty that grew most rapidly in the sudden evolutionary expansion of our own brain capacity.

There is one even more surprising aspect to the discrimination of pattern by functional geometry: certain kinds of patterns will always be selected out as unique or primitive patterns by any mosaic system, whether biological or artificial. While a mathematician of curved spaces might say that an S-curve in one curved space is a straight line in another and that these are equally good descriptions, a functional mosaic will accept as straight only those Euclidean lines that satisfy self-congruence under displacement.

This selectivity means that an external characteristic called straightness is a primitive and unique category of perception to all such mosaic systems. Likewise something called parallelism, and something called equidistance, and so on. There are other important categories of perception such as continuity and discreteness which contribute to "thingness" but which will not concern us here; in part they involve the local self-congruence of small areas of the input pattern rather than the larger symmetry. It is interesting to see that these various categories are the "synthetic *a priori*" categories of Kant, and some of them are the "unprovable axioms of science" of Bertrand Russell—unique categories that impose themselves on all minds regardless of particular experiences and yet cannot be learned without particular experiences and comparisons.

I suspect that there is only a small number of these unique symmetry categories for a visual mosaic receptor, and that these are just the complete set of "group-theoretical" operations involving the three rotations of the eyeball. (The "group theory" referred to is the mathematical theory of the rotations and other operations about a point center that transform a symmetrical pattern from one configuration into another one identical to it.) If so, every visual pattern relationship that can be perceived is some combination of these rotation operations associated with the group theory. To take an example, consider three lines that are not equidistant but are separated by distances in the ratio $1:\pi$, where π is the irrational number 3.1415. One might ask whether such a set of lines could ever form a natural or primitive pattern category for all minds—perhaps to be distinguished and identified by a sophisticated self-congruence of the intervals under some queer combination of motions. I think the answer is that a *genetic* system might be evolved to select such a pattern, or any other; but that such a pattern would not satisfy self-congruence for any imaginable mosaic receptor whatever. "God made the integers, man made all the rest" is the remark of a big mosaic receptor that looks for sharp boundaries and self-congruence.

In the one dimension belonging to time, there is only one self-congruent pattern element. It is repetition or periodicity, like that of a rhythmic beat or, on a finer scale, that of the successive waves in a steady tone. We know, of course, that very complex rhythmic patterns can be combined, but it will scarcely be denied that the pattern variation available to composers is far less than the two-dimensional and three-dimensional variation available to the painter or sculptor.

These remarks on the physics of perception can be reduced to two main points. First, time and space fluctuations of input stimuli are probably necessary in order to perceive pattern, at least in the learning stage. Second, a big mosaic detector preferentially selects as unique just those few pattern elements that have the self-congruence property in space or time.

I think we can extend both principles from the area of perception to the area of appreciation. There is a physiological component in all satisfaction: one can't enjoy anything with a stomach ache. The brain is a physiological organ. It would be hard to believe that any physiological process that goes as far back in evolution as does the acquisition and ordering of new information should not have the strongest affective overtones in our daily lives. The functional satisfaction that comes from this large organ doing its job and doing it well may be a major element in our feelings of pleasure and aesthetic satisfaction.

If this is so, then at the root of enjoyment must lie the same factors that perception itself depends upon. If fluctuations are basic to perception, we may suspect that they will play a large role in enjoyment. If the self-congruent patterns are basic for perception, we may suspect they will be basic for enjoyment. And perhaps a combination of the two, a flux in which we can find a pattern, or a pattern that contains unexpected fluctuations, will give the greatest satisfaction of all. The child is pleased and laughs when, in his random scanning up and down a line, he discovers straightness or, in his manipulation of the block, he discovers that it just fits the hole in the box. Perhaps the intellectual satisfaction of the adult has the same roots. This could help us understand why all the students in a mathematics class are pleased by an elegant proof, a proof that uses the full reasoning and inductive powers of the brain to discover a new order in a maze of complexity.

ART AND THE SYMMETRIES
OF ANIMALS

The mathematician and group theorist, Hermann Weyl, in his classic essay on "Symmetry" discusses the translational and rotational symmetry groups used by artists. He pays especial attention to the symmetry forms found in the biological world, forms which are basic points of departure for painters and sculptors. In fact, all of us are accustomed to certain symmetries throughout our lives just because of our experience of the animal world.

In these forms, only certain symmetry classes are found. For example, many single-cell animals, spores, blood cells, and other free-floating creatures which seem indifferent to propulsion in one direction rather than another, are spherical or quasi-spherical, with a shape indifferent to direction in space. They are self-congruent under rotation. We are immediately in the presence of art as well as geometry. This is exactly the reason why the Greeks spoke of the sphere and the circle as the most perfect shapes, although the classical geometry that defines these shapes by points and fixed radii tends to obscure the self-congruence property.

Angular shapes have a lower symmetry. They have some self-congruence under directional changes, but of a more limited kind. An angular figure that can be converted into itself only by certain discrete rotations has the symmetry of a polygon; or, in three dimensions, of a polyhedron. This lower, but still very great, symmetry is seen in the beautiful star polyhedra of the radiolarians. It is also seen in the art of Christmas ornaments, which are free-swinging if not free-floating, and are therefore free to have space symmetry rather than flat symmetry. In animals where one might expect rotational indifference, the choice between round and angular forms probably depends on whether their mode of life requires minimum surface area (round) or maximum surface area (pointed) for survival.

Moving up the scale of life, the sessile animals or plants that are attached to a surface tend to have cylindrical symmetry, with a shape indifferent to rotation about an axis perpendicular to the surface, and therefore self-congruent under this rotation. We see this in sea anemones and sand dollars and in the general shapes of trees and their trunks. A few moving forms with directed motions, especially swimming or burrowing forms, are also relatively indifferent to rotation about the axis of motion and have cylindrical symmetry, like that of roundworms and the roots of plants. Self-congruence under discrete rotations about an axis gives us the polygonal forms of the starfish and of flowers.

For plants climbing on vertical surfaces, gravity and light give a preferred direction along the surface and the cylindrical symmetry is lost. The same is true for animals having a directed motion over a surface, that is, having a head end and a tail end. For such forms, there is only one possible symmetry remaining, bilateral symmetry, which means indifference to right and left, or to reflection in a plane perpendicular to the surface and containing the head-tail axis. Reflection is a group-theoretical operation not available to the rotating eyeball, so we are not terribly sensitive to right-left differences or to deviations from symmetry in our friends' faces. As a result, familiar faces look strange when seen in a mirror. But we are sensitive to equidistance; and perhaps it is the equidistance of the right and left sides of an object from the median line that accounts for whatever abstract appreciation of bilateral symmetry we have.

In nature we also find the symmetry of equidistant segments, or, technically, periodic translational self-congruence. It is everywhere in the lower animals and plants, in the segments of the bamboo or the worm, in the legs of the millipede and in the nipples of the pig. A similar symmetry is screw symmetry or the helical translational-rotational periodicity, which is found at the molecular level in long-chain protein and nucleic acid molecules, and higher up, in helical plant stems and spiral shells, as emphasized by D'Arcy Thompson in his seminal book, *On Growth and Form*. But these translational and helical repetitions of form do not grow out of the symmetry relations to the environment as the rotation symmetries do. Our own bodies have no visible helical periodicities, I believe, except in kinky hair, and no translational periodicities except in hidden or small parts such as ribs and vertebrae, fingers and toes, eyelashes, and fingerprints.

The strange and interesting thing about self-congruence relations is that there are no other symmetry classes than those we have mentioned. One can say with mathematical certainty that the Martians or creatures from any other world must have either some of these symmetries, or none!

(Psychologists might consider adding other symmetry groups to the Rorschach ink blot test. The monotonous bilateral symmetry of these tests necessarily tends to lead to interpretations involving animal forms. If subjects were presented with fivefold symmetries, or translational periodicities, or representations of three-dimensional circular symmetries, the variety of the interpretations might be greatly increased.)

To summarize these remarks on pattern, there is evidently a happy coincidence between many of the physiological symmetries imposed by evolution and the primitive pattern symmetries involved in perception. Weyl emphasizes this agreement. Both of these symmetries have a common geometrical explanation. The reason is that they are both derived from the limited set of group-theory symmetries of the "translation groups" and "rotation groups" in three dimensions. We can go on to see that this coincidence of the two sets of forms makes them doubly significant for us as elements of artistic organization, because they now have *both* a referential and a formal meaning, and in art they satisfy us on two levels at once, the biological and the abstract. That is to say, the bizarre fascination of fences and lattices and the repetitious windows of Italian palaces is related on the one hand to the familiar biological repetition of the centipede and the spinal column and on the other hand to the importance of equidistance in our own visual organization of space.

Similar remarks would apply to the time dimension. Repetition and time-periodicity, which are the self-congruent categories of temporal perceptual organization, are also the categories of biological sounds and rhythmic biological movement. We perhaps should recognize that they also can satisfy us on two levels and can have some referential meaning as well as a formal meaning when they appear in the temporal arts of music and the abstract screen. The biological and emotional meaning of a fast tempo is necessarily different from that of a slow one, even if the formal pattern is exactly the same.

The intention of this discussion of symmetry has been to show that there could reasonably be within us a physiological basis for calling certain geometrical symmetry relations beautiful. It is now time to go further and to emphasize that the connection between mathematical pattern and aesthetic excellence has been, in fact, a central part of aesthetic criticism since the dawn of history. In all our languages, the technical terms that indicate geometrical or physical regularities are also the terms of artistic praise. Ever since the Greeks, the words balance, symmetry, and harmony have had both meanings.

A symmetrical picture is well balanced. Musical harmonics are harmonious. Harmony in the laboratory is a numerical relation between frequencies; outside, it is a larger aesthetic satisfaction. Rhythm is even used occasionally in the larger sense, as in describing smooth and skillful movements, or the good life. I mention these linguistic identities not as an argument, but as a deep psychological summary of many arguments. For two thousand years, mathematical regularities have been inseparable from the aesthetic dialogue.

THE NEED FOR DEVIATIONS
IN PATTERNS

Modern aesthetic theory says, nevertheless, that formal beauty is more than pattern: what is beautiful is pattern that contains uncertainty and surprise and yet resolves them into the regularity of a larger pattern. I believe that this view can easily be understood in the light of our physiological need for novelty as well as pattern. Long-lasting aesthetic satisfaction is produced not by one pattern by itself, for this soon becomes boring, but only by a pattern developing into patterns of patterns, continually full of new information drawing attention to itself.

This is a change from older ideas. Weyl admits, for example, that ". . . occidental art, like life itself, is inclined to mitigate, to loosen, to modify, even to break strict symmetry." But he then asserts, "Even in asymmetric designs one feels symmetry as the norm from which one deviates under the influence of forces of non-formal character." As part of a thesis on symmetry, this is excellent, but as criticism, it is incomplete. In current theory, the deviation is as important to art as the norm, and we may have formal statistically random forces as well as nonformal ones, plus, of course, those deviations which turn out to be components of larger forms.

Again, Weyl says, "All musicians agree that underlying the emotional element of music is a strong formal element. It may be that it is capable of some such mathematical treatment as has proved successful for the art of ornaments." True. And we have seen how the emotion might be generated. But a more complete statement would include the strong emotions produced by formal randomness, like the emotions of gamblers or of children playing peek-a-boo, and would also include the possibility of a mathematical treatment of randomness or information content as well as of order. We want a theme with variations; and the variations are as important as the theme.

In the word "attractive" there is another double meaning that illustrates this point. The attractive (from Latin *trahere*, to draw) signifies not only an aesthetic judgment but also a physical pull: that which draws us, that which our eyes "trace" and follow; the unusual, the information-full. A moving spot on the landscape, a memorable design, or a strange perfume draws or attracts us through basic feedback mechanisms of great importance for survival and therefore of great emotional importance. It is a question of the singular case. Put one fly in a classroom and the whole class watches it. Put a hundred in, and no one bothers. Everyone remembers the audience-rousing blare that precedes the "Hymn to Joy" in the Ninth Symphony, because it is so singular and unexpected; and later on, so triumphantly resolved. The classic aesthetic formulations are incomplete: What is memorable is not the perfect but the perfect that contains the unexpected. "There is no excellent beauty that hath not some strangeness in the proportions," said Bacon. He was the first of the moderns.

Several critics have described this link, in music and poetry, between aesthetic emotion and new information. Among the humanists, Leonard Meyer may come closest to thinking in terms of quantitative information theory. He says, in discussing value and greatness in music:

> At one time I subscribed to I. A. Richard's statement that "the two pillars upon which a theory of criticism must rest are an account of value and an account of communication." However it has seemed increasingly clear that these two are as inextricably linked to each other as are means and ends. When you discuss one, you are of necessity implying the other.

And he stresses elsewhere "the importance of uncertainty in musical communication, the probabilistic nature of musical style." In his book on *Emotion and Meaning in Music,* he shows how composers manipulate our expectations and thereby surprise us in order to achieve an aesthetic effect. When we listen to music, he says,

> Under certain conditions we expect change, under others continuity, and under still others repetition . . . expectation is always ahead of the music, creating a background of diffuse tension against which particular delays articulate the affective curve and create meaning.

A detailed musical analysis along these lines would not be easy to describe here. But it is easy to see what Meyer means if we apply his ideas to the development of a simple visual pattern, the kind of thing we might watch developing in a television advertisement. Suppose I draw an incomplete circle for you, thus:

You watch it and wait for me to finish it, in a sense completing it in your mind. There is a hesitation and a sense of tension in you while waiting, like the sense of tension in waiting for the second shoe to fall in the apartment overhead. When the circle is finally completed there is at least a little sense of satisfaction.

But suppose I start over and draw only part of the circle:

and then while you are waiting for me to complete it, I draw instead a similar part of another circle, a mirror image, a little distance away so that the two gaps face each other. As the second circle is begun, there is a moment of confusion and then the expectation of

the first is postponed. There is a reassessment. You think, Aha! Maybe he will stop at the same point on the second one; then there would be some symmetry. And when I do stop at that point, you feel that expectation satisfied; but the other expectation of completion now reappears more intensely than before, because there are now two circles to be completed.

Yet if I simply do complete them, I am sure you will feel a let-

down. That would simply satisfy your old expectation; and you have now begun to like this game of having a little uncertainty at every step about what the new development will be.

So the situation of the two circles with gaps cries out for a different solution, for a third entity to be developed, a third movement in musical terms. And if we do not want to build up great contrapuntal designs—which would be interesting and which might be the great abstract screen art of the future—then a simple solution is to draw a third complete circle symmetrically between the other two, touching and so closing the four open points.

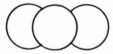

This last addition to the two circles with gaps surprises us in a certain sense, by not fulfilling the initial expectations at all. Yet it satisfies the expectation of closure as well as that of novelty by producing closure in another way. And the closure is particularly satisfying because it is a closure in several senses at once. As the last circle is just being completed, it restores the symmetry which has been temporarily disrupted during the drawing of it, it closes itself, and it closes the first two, all at the same time. It brings them all together in a larger architectonic unity, to use the grand musical terminology. We have a feeling of completion, a feeling that any further pencil stroke would necessarily have to be a starting off of some completely new idea.

The completed pattern I have drawn is a rather standard design motif, suitable perhaps for a beer advertisement or for a new Olympic flag. As a television ad, of course, the final architectonic triumph would turn out to be the manufacturer's trademark. People get paid for composing this kind of game; and millions watch, so it must be aesthetically satisfying to somebody, perhaps for some of the reasons just outlined.

The same teasing game can be found in music, if one looks for it. Anyone can work out for himself the similar structure of an immortal nursery tune like "Three Blind Mice," with its expectations, little fulfillments, surprises, and so on. By the time you reach the end of it, you are astonished to catalog how many different kinds of chromatic and rhythmic expectation are satisfied by the concluding descending phrase.

In *Emotion and Meaning in Music,* Meyer emphasizes that our expectations in a given art medium are built up culturally. If the playing of "Three Blind Mice" were interrupted at one point or another, a Western six-year-old child with a good ear and some musical experience could probably pick out many of the next fulfillment-notes on a piano, even if he had not heard the tune before (if such a combination of experience and musical naïveté is possible in our society). But a comparable Senegalese child or a Chinese child, from a different culture with a different musical scale, probably could not do this nearly as well, except perhaps for the identification of the universal keynote at the end. On the other hand, these other children would have expectations for their own music that we would be unable to guess. This is what makes Oriental and African music difficult for Westerners to understand or enjoy. It violates our expectations at almost every note, so that our perception of the organization is slow and difficult, like the attempt of a visually naïve adult to perceive a triangle.

In a later paper, Meyer illustrates the aesthetic necessity for variation of pattern by comparing two similar themes with a similar basic melody, one by Bach (the introductory bars of the Prelude and Fugue for Organ), and one by Geminiani. The first is better, Meyer says, because Bach introduces unexpected variations, where Geminiani simply descends straight down the scale, so that there is less delay in our expectation, and less satisfaction when we reach the end. The circle is completed, but too easily. He loses our attention because he plays no games with us.

This may be a good place to mention the relation of these notions to games and amusement. It is music, I believe, that proves the fundamental nature of humor more conclusively than all the books that have been written explaining humor. For it is an experimental fact that the formal patterns of music and their variations can be not only amusing in the sense of being entertaining but amusing in the sense of being laughable. Whole audiences can be made to laugh on cue at the Surprise Symphony or at Mozart's off-key violin. This is not referential humor; no external clown is being pointed to and the amusement is not produced by funny glubbing noises from the oboe or tuba. It is formal internal humor having to do with the syntax of the musical sentence, with some combination of delay-and-fulfillment or doubt-and-reassurance as the shocking gaffe is found to be part of a larger plan. Not pattern, but surprise-in-pattern. The explosion of breath is the physiological proof of our tension and relief. It might help our understanding if we called this pattern-game "wit" and made a sharp distinction between it and "humor." Wit is syntactic, humor referential.

What has complicated the interpretation of laughter is the referential character of most humor: the conceited man who slips on a banana peel. But this has formal humor also. Surprise, that an adult should fall; satisfaction, that his conceit has fallen also, to where it belongs. We say that man is the only animal that laughs. This means he is the only animal that plays games with patterns. The child will laugh at patterns that give only a gentle pleasure to adults. Perhaps all the child's games are such a mixture of formal patterns and surprise. But the roots of the adult's pleasure are in the child's laughter.

Music is a good field in which to study this interaction between the regular and the unexpected, the shock and the reevaluation, with their resultant aesthetic—or humorous—effects. It is a one-dimensional form, so that a complete analysis is easier than for the multidimensional forms of the colored visual arts with their tremendous information inputs. Reproduction and playback are simple, and the investigator could stop a musical piece and determine, as Shannon did for language, the precise statistical expectations of an audience, thus actually measuring quantitatively the information conveyed by the next notes. And the investigator can examine easily the aesthetic effect of various alternatives.

Pseudomusic is already being written by computing machines, as Hiller and Isaacson have described. The machine chooses random notes for its compositions, imposing on them only the rules of harmony and those short-range correlations between successive notes which are typical, say, of a culture or of a particular composer. It is rather startling to find that by this simple means, the machine produces a crude but recognizable imitation of the style in question. Eventually such an experimental approach will permit the effects of randomness and pattern choices, both long-range and short-range, to be studied in detail. Perhaps a computing machine, if it knew enough about what to expect, could even write a Surprise Symphony. It would be interesting to find out whether it could be programmed to have a sense of humor! At any rate, work with computing machine compositions is going to enable music teachers and composers to get a clearer understanding of the ground rules of their craft. Music may soon become, if it is not already, the most sophisticated field of aesthetic criticism.

EXCELLENCE IN POETRY

Finally, it is interesting to examine a few quotations that show the same ideas running through modern poetic criticism. The first one is a very explicit statement by Gerard Manley Hopkins, who influenced so many later poets. In a kind of undergraduate manifesto, "On the Origin of Beauty: A Platonic Dialogue" (in the journals and papers edited by House and Storey) he applies to poetry his own theory of natural and visual beauty, which is summarized in these words:

> "Then the beauty of the oak and the chestnut-fan and the sky is a mixture of likeness and difference, or agreement and disagreement, or consistency and variety, or symmetry and change."

> "It seems so, yes."

> "And if we did not feel the likeness we should not think them so beautiful, or if we did not feel the difference we should not think them so beautiful. The beauty we find is from the comparison we make of the things with themselves, seeing their likeness and difference, is it not?"

Hopkins then applies this to rhythm in poetry.

> ". . . Rhythm therefore is likeness tempered with difference . . . And the beauty of rhythm is traced to the same causes as that of the chestnut-fan, is it not so?"

And he extends this to other aspects of poetic beauty in considerable detail.

It is also instructive to note this passage from Aristotle, on rhythm in prose, which Hopkins singles out for quotation in his later lecture notes on rhythm and rhetoric:

> The shape (or figure) of the diction must not be metrical nor yet unrhythmical. The first of these breeds distrust: it seems artificial and moreover it stands out and catches the ear, making the hearer on the watch for resemblances, when the chime will come again . . . On the other hand what is unrhythmical is unbounded. Now it should be bounded . . .

I think that this requirement that art should "not be metrical" is an insight unusual in Greek criticism. But it is coming to be common in modern poetic theory, as shown in the following quotation by Meyer from Robert Penn Warren.

> . . . a poem, to be good, must earn itself. It is a motion toward a point of rest, but if it is not a resisted motion, it is a motion of no consequence. For example, a poem which depends upon stock materials and stock responses is simply a toboggan slide, or a fall through space.

One thinks of the fall through space of the Geminiani theme.

In the same vein, someone else has said of Longfellow's style: "If you try to write poetry in the regular meter of 'By the shores of Gitchee Gumee, by the shining Big-Sea-Water,' you might as well write prose." The audience becomes bored; and something variable,

some new information, has to be introduced just to maintain attention, even before one can begin to achieve any emotional response.

John Crowe Ransom says, in *The World's Body:*

> It is not merely easy for a technician to write in smooth
> metres; it is perhaps easier than to write in rough ones, after he
> has once started; but when he has written smoothly, and con-
> templates the work, he is capable actually, if he is a modern
> poet, of going over it laboriously and roughening it.

Naturally, what is rough and what is smooth depends upon our
expectations. "A rose is a rose is a rose" is a repetition, but far from
smooth or expected. What we expect is a predicate definition. The
most interesting predicate could not be such a surprise. Each "rose"
means something different—in the sense of formal, not referential,
meaning—because each satisfies or surprises with respect to a different expectation. The second "rose" is rare but possible, a blunt, fac-
tual emphasis; we do "call a spade a spade." But the third one
builds it up into the easy pattern of a child's chant; which for an
adult is a linguistic outrage. The trivial repetition is so incredible
that it becomes immortal, and changes every "rose" forever after.

T. S. Eliot explicitly compares poetic organization to musical
organization. In an essay on *The Music of Poetry,* he says:

> There are possibilities for verse which bear some analogy
> to the development of a theme by different groups of instru-
> ments; there are possibilities of transitions in a poem compara-
> ble to the different movements of a symphony or a quartet;
> there are possibilities of contrapuntal arrangement of subject
> matter.

So a theory which accounts for the aesthetic satisfaction of the one
form may be applicable to the other also.

Another passage of Eliot's describes particularly clearly the
need for both pattern and change in poetry. He says in his early
essay, "Reflections on *Vers Libre":*

> . . . the most interesting verse which has yet been written
> in our language has been done either by taking a very simple
> form, like the iambic pentameter, and constantly withdrawing
> from it, or taking no form at all, and constantly approximating
> to a very simple one. It is this contrast between fixity and flux,
> this unperceived evasion of monotony, which is the very life of
> verse.

This brings us full circle, back to the text from Eliot that I
quoted at the beginning. Perhaps it is now less of a riddle. Poetry is
like "amusement," because of its "surprise" and abstract "elevation."

It is amusing because it is like wit or humor, which, as we saw for pure musical wit, depends on surprise combined with fulfillment. Our highest mental organization is a continual search for patterns and surprises.

This modern insistence on pattern variation may go beyond anything the Greek critics demanded of their art. In poetics as in music and architecture and science today, we may be reaching out for organizational complexities not dreamed of earlier. We are realizing that it is amusement in this larger sense that is the present intellectual and aesthetic demand.

"But if we think of anything else that poetry"—or wit, or any other art—"may seem to be, we are led into far greater difficulties."

SHAPING

V

Communication and Collective Choice

In a high-interaction society, all of us must have a say in decisions that affect our destiny.

COMMUNICATION MEANS INTERACTION. And high-intensity communications, such as we have today increasingly all over the world, necessarily mean high-intensity interactions. This is a basic reason for many of the new tensions and conflicts that have developed across the world in the last few years.

It is worth thinking about these relationships for a moment. Etymologically, "communing" means "sharing *with* one another." Nevertheless, it is easy to think of many kinds of supposed communication we have today which are not sharing *with* us, and which are not *inter*action. The communication is not with us, but at us. We speak of our "communications media," but the kind of television in which somebody out there has organized a program, and is throwing it at me, the kind in which I can't talk back or have my side represented, this is not communication. In some ways, it is more like excommunication.

It seems to me that there are an enormous number of aspects of modern life where we speak of the "communications media" when we ought to use some different word, some word which means "throwing stuff at you." It seems to me this is one of the central reasons for the alienation of our times. We are alienated because we are treated as alienated. We are treated as not worthy or not ready for participation in the communications process in a sense of *"with."*

Sometimes our attempts to communicate with each other are like the story about the boy who had a date with a fat girl, and his mother said, "Jimmy, try to find something nice to say about her." So he thought and he thought all evening, and he finally came up with: "Gee, you don't sweat much for a fat girl."

In many of our interactions with our supposed leaders, or our elites, or our media, or with each other—or interactions that should be with each other—the talker is about as far from the other party as Jimmy was from the fat girl. He was saying something nice in his terms, but he was not identifying very well with her problem.

So it seems to me, today, that when we have "communications" —so-called—about ghetto riots, for example, who is it that comes in with the TV cameras? It is not members of the ghetto. Who writes the articles on it for the newspapers? It is not members of the ghetto. The cameras, the stories, report on them as "they." "They" did it.

In the same way, when we have teacher-parent confrontations, all too often the teachers are saying "they" about the parents, while the parents are saying "they" about the teachers. And when we have a story on hippies, it is "they" who have the funny clothes. And when we have a dialogue on the question of what length of hair is to be allowed by students in the high schools, it is "they" who have that funny, long hair.

When we are blocked from sharing in this way, the pressure to *com*municate on some other channel finally becomes very great. It is only human nature to come back, to be seen and heard, in some other way. So the rules of Parliament and the Congress in treating the opponents as "Honorable" members—who also have a microphone and may be listened to—reduce tension because they permit real communication.

Something like this can be done, and surely will be done, whenever we want to dampen hostilities. One of the remarkable moments in the 1968 campaign came when Senator Muskie was being heckled by a crowd, and he suddenly asked the crowd to choose one of their number to come up and take the platform with the microphone; and the boy came up and talked for several minutes with the communications medium in *his* hand. This is one of the few times in our recent confrontations, when for a few moments we didn't have "they." Instead, we had "we," with a dialogue together. We must find ways to make this happen in more of our confrontations.

In international relations, there is a similar problem between the great powers of the world and the nations that call themselves the "third world." The great powers push their pawns about the map, and push their military force and their economic force into many places, saying: "They will be benefited by a new road, or by a new dam, by a new population solution." And, accordingly, the third world responds, as you might expect, by saying: "It is not our dam, it is their dam. 'They' did it. 'They' are responsible for how things are happening."

When things go like this, real communication is replaced by obstruction. All of us today are falling far short of the idea that real communication is interaction. Many of our troubles come from this. But, I also think that there is great hope in the last few years simply because in every city and country we are demanding more of this real communication, more of a say, more dialogue, and more negotiation. Mothers are lying down in front of the bulldozers, because this is their only way of saying effectively that "they" in City Hall cannot obliterate this block or this park until the people involved have had something to say about it.

John Seeley has defined "poverty" as "the inability to command events that affect your destiny." This describes not only monetary poverty. It also defines intellectual poverty, and it defines political poverty—the inability to affect events that will determine your destiny.

In this sense, what we are seeing today is a great cry in an affluent society for us to be poor no more. It is a cry for us to communicate and affect and be affected. It is a cry for the teachers to be taught by the students, and a cry for the parents to be taught by the children. Throughout history, teachers have found that they are in fact better teachers and more successful teachers, if instead of having a wall of armor around them which says "I will teach you so and so," they say, "I have no armor. I am willing to learn and have an openness to what the child can teach me."

And the child does have things to teach, to communicate to the teacher. He has resources which we have often forgotten, resources of spontaneity, resources of living-in-the-present, of seeing things as they are, resources of joy, of humor, which adults grown dull and harried need to learn again from the children.

It is striking to look around and to see an occasional adult who still has this kind of openness to the child, this willingness to be taught as well as to teach. And it is striking to see how such an adult comes to be surrounded by children and comes to be particularly effective when he does teach.

With such a person, the children suddenly don't say: " 'They' are making us do tenth grade work." They say: " 'We're going to do tenth grade work." They don't say: "The teachers have planned a party, or the principal is going to plan a party." They say: " 'We are going to plan a party." Now life, and education, is not all advancement, and not all parties—although the best education, when it is getting across, comes to seem like pleasure and advancement all the time. Nevertheless, the parents or the teachers whose children have come to say "*We* are going to do something," have already made an enormous step forward. It is a sign that there is communication that is going both ways, that is becoming 'with'-ness and sharing.

But none of us are responsive enough—and that includes myself as well. For years, as an administrator, I had a great steel desk, until I began to realize that I was using it as my body armor. It was standing between me and the student who came in, or the man who wanted an adjustment in his salary, or even the person who just wanted to talk. And when I realized that this was constantly turning me into the kind of person I did not want to be, I threw the desk out—and now the office has two chairs in it, which are not more than six feet apart, and a rug that I went and bought. (My State institution isn't quite ready yet to buy a rug for someone so low on the totem pole.) The rubber-tiled floor was a mark of pre-1960 industrial efficiency and economy. It was a mark that I was in an automatic institution with an administrative hierarchy, and I thought the communication, the personal with-sharing, would flow back and forth more easily across that rug than across the rubber-tiled floor.

And suddenly it seemed to me that just the act of throwing out the desk and getting the rug began to make me a different person. Whether the effect was on me or was on the people who came in, suddenly it felt like there was a new warmth of interaction— although I realize that an administrator can never be quite certain. But, whether this particular attempt succeeded or not, each of us needs to look for ways of taking away his physical or psychological armor so that he can have a "with" relation to other people.

Today, our new picture of perception and of communication is bringing us around on a scientific basis to Martin Buber's point of view. Buber said, "We do not see 'its', but 'I–its'." Our relation to the objects of the world is an interaction relation, which is what the perception story has told us.

And in these same terms I think we can begin to understand the next stage of Buber's dialogue. We do not see "Thou"—that is, the other person as an isolated object. Instead, we have and we must have, an "I-Thou" relation. We have not really seen the other person until the other person has also seen us and interacted with us. Communication is interaction.

Donald Mackay, the British perception theorist, has discussed the logical possibility, or rather the impossibility, of predicting another person's behavior in a rigorous scientific sense. The difficulty is partly because the brain is so complex. Its complexity is so far beyond the complexities of everything else we know, all put together, that it is almost inconceivable. Nevertheless, Mackay says that the real reason why we cannot predict the behavior of other people is not a physical difficulty but a logical difficulty. The real reason is that we are *communicating* with the other person; and the other person becomes unpredictable because our communication makes him a part of ourselves. We are members, one of another.

This is really a generalization of the well-known fact that I cannot predict my own behavior in a scientific sense. For example, suppose I predict that I will wear a red tie tomorrow morning, and I try to make a bet with you on it, and I say, "Come on, bet me a dollar that I won't wear a red tie tomorrow morning." You will just laugh at me; and rightly so, because, clearly, whichever way you bet, it affects my behavior, and so my behavior is not independent of the bet. My behavior is not independent of my prediction. Prediction is not scientific or deterministic prediction, except in an objective world or an "isolated system" where we take away our hands from the experiment and let it run its course without interacting with it. When we do that, we can predict in a deterministic way, more or less accurately, what will happen, but you cannot predict in this scientific sense your own behavior. Your statement is not, technically, a prediction but an *intention,* which you can revise at any time, because you interact so strongly with what you say you are going to do.

In the same sense, a prediction of what another person will do is also not a scientific prediction, according to Mackay—because the other person is a communicating person. If you predict to a ball that it will fall, your prediction will not affect the ball's falling. But if you predict to a man that he will fall, he may be more careful to stay upright just to violate your prediction, or he may fall more comically just to make it true.

THE PARTICIPATING SOCIETY

So the reason we cannot predict other people's behavior is because we are interacting with them all the time. And one sees immediately that in this same sense one cannot predict the behavior of a society, because the very basis of society is communication-interaction. A single act in the brain of a single individual can change the

whole future of the world. We all know this, really. We know it because of assassins, but it is also true for inventors, or for political or
intellectual leaders of any kind. An inventor gets a new idea, a new
concept, a new way of making an airplane, or a new way of making
atomic energy. Or he makes the "mistake" of using *this* detection
device rather than that one, and so discovers a new physical principle which otherwise would not have been discovered for five more
years. And the effects of such inventions or discoveries sweep across
continents. The same is true of an act of leadership; when a man
suddenly stands up and says, like Thoreau, "I am marching to a different drum," men hear this and the whole future of a country may
be changed. So there are acts in individual brains which affect the
whole future of society because we are an intercommunicating
group. And in this sense the future of society cannot be predicted
any more accurately or scientifically than my own future, as in the
question of whether I am going to wear a red tie tomorrow or not.

This strong interaction is the basis of our despair, but it is also
the basis of our hope. Because now we can go back and consider
Skinner's powerful methods of shaping behavior and we can say,
"Let us now take action to shape each other's behavior by our mutual desire and will, by our responsibility as teachers and parents,
not by predictions but by interactions, by cybernetic goal-seeking,
in directions we choose and want."

Thinking of our own interaction with it, in fact we see that the
future of society is something that *we* decide, that *we* determine,
as leaders and inventors—yes, and as non-cooperators and assassins, unfortunately—in a kind of collective way at each moment. I can only conclude that today we may become and are
becoming, in a sense that we have never been in the history of man,
a self-conscious communicative society, a participating society.

For a long time, I used to ask, what does our new phrase "participatory democracy" mean, except just democracy? Two hundred
years ago our forefathers brought forth the idea that there should
be a "representative democracy" in this country. The idea was that
everybody should participate in selecting their representatives and
public officials. But today we realize that the new idea of participatory democracy does not simply concern elections of officials; it concerns the administrative decisions of those public officials between
elections, to make sure they are not simply pushing people about
for their own class purposes or administrative convenience. It is no
longer enough for us to go to the polls and cast our ballots. We also
want to be consulted. We do not want to be treated any longer as

objects, in that objective world we talked about. We want to be treated as co-subjects, in a subjective world, not manipulated by an elite, but instead shared with as a group, a group which is collectively determining its own decisions.

The history of Western man could be written as the history of the elites who have determined our destinies. The first elite was, of course, the aristocrats, the kings and the barons, the feudal lords. By and by feudalism went out, and commercial society came in, and the elite came to be the great capitalists. In the last century, one still knew their names—Gould, Vanderbilt, Morgan, Carnegie.

Today, one can hardly name the names of the heads of the great American corporations. (It is an interesting challenge to try on yourself or your intellectual friends!) The reason is that it is no longer individual capitalists who are our elites, determining our destiny. It is now committees of managers, or what John Galbraith has called the "technostructure."

But today, we are moving beyond even this method of guiding society. We are now realizing our own demand that we must not have our lives determined even by committees of managers—even though they may be somewhat more democratic and more broadly based and more expert than the older individualist capitalists. For, even with committees of managers, it is still "they" against "us." Even if we are the lowest sweepers on the floor of the corporation, we want to have some kind of say in our destiny, and we form unions. Even if we are the students in the school, we want to have some kind of say about whether we can have cars, or wear our hair long, or entertain girls in our rooms, or what kind of courses we are taught, or what kind of changes the administration will cooperate with us in making.

The lesson of our times is this new demand for a kind of collective formation of our own future. If we look at history, we realize that in every age, the new needs, and the new situation of the age, lead to a demand for new rights. At one time these new rights were represented by Magna Charta, at another time they came to include the right to vote, or the right not to be a slave, or the right of votes for women, or the right to unionize.

It seems to me that the new rights for which a demand is arising in our time, I think in an irresistible way, revolve primarily around *the right not to be treated as an object*. We are co-subjects in our society. We want the right to have a choice among the varied programs. We want an "ombudsman" to keep us from being pushed around by administrators. We want the right to have a choice about whether the bulldozers will push over our buildings and our parks. We want the right not to be lied to by doctors and officials; not to be betrayed by counselors, not to be manipulated by elites who present us with a fait accompli for city planning or for education—we want the right to take part in the decisions that affect the destinies of all of us.

It is a kind of "collective existentialism" for us all. The existentialist starts off, of course, from existential despair. He starts from the realization that he can commit suicide at any moment. This is his freedom. He can jump out the window. He can destroy everything that has made him up to that instant. But from this basis of existential despair, there is no place to go but up. This means that he is also free to make existential choices and actions which affect his future; choices of what education he will have; choices of what wife he will choose; choices of whether to have children; choices of how to build a house or a city or how to lead a people.

The existentialist is confronted with the freedom which begins with the right to commit suicide, and ends with the right to shape his own future anew at every moment.

I think the world today is in a situation of "collective existentialism." We are faced with terrible problems, and many of us are ready to opt out. Some of these problems involve a kind of collective lunacy of throwing nuclear weapons at each other; or a kind of collective madness of a large nation trying to tell a smaller nation what kind of government to have, whether this is on one side of the Iron Curtain or the other.

And yet, at the same time, there is a demand for a collective right to shape our own future in new ways, to move into the Twenty-first century with new patterns of sharing and democratic participation in such a way that none of us are poor any longer. In any way.

The new world can only come into being if we find a better way for all of us to have a say in the manifold decisions which are to determine our destiny.

VI

Shaping the Evolutionary Future

There will be more human evolution in the next 50 years than in the last 100,000.—Joshua Lederberg

TODAY, great changes are taking place in our ways of life all over the world. They are almost certainly the most sudden and widespread and dramatic changes that have occurred in any generation in the history of mankind. A one-hundred-year-old man today will have lived through the coming of the telephone, the electric light, the automobile, the airplane, the motion picture, and the radio, not to speak of television, nylon, atomic energy, space travel, oral contraceptives, and such principles of social organization as Communism and the pay-as-you-go income tax.

Yet these changes are not merely technological and social changes. In a broad sense they are also biological. For one thing, they grow out of man's biology. Our greatest achievements in science or in large-scale social organization are shaped by biological demands and emotions and the tissue structure within the human skull. They depend on our curiosity, speech, and reasoning, and on our ability or inability to teach, to learn, to plan, and to work together with other men. But at the same time, these new developments also react back and change man's biology, for they affect his foods and drugs, his houses and habitats, his health and diseases, his population pressures and wars, and his interrelations with the rest of mankind and with all the rest of the biological world of plants and animals that he multiplies or destroys.

Biology and technology have interacted before. What we are seeing is only a modern counterpart of the prehistoric invention of tools, fire, and speech, which occurred, it is estimated, something like two million years ago. It appears that the effort of living with these inventions may be what lengthened man's period of learning in childhood, and what fed and forced the steady enlargment of his

119

brain, until today it is three times its original size. It was these inventions that began to make man human.

Today—in the last twenty thousand years, the last two thousand years, the last four hundred years, the last one hundred years, the last twenty-five years—as we see changes piled upon changes, it is hard to believe that they are not pressing us toward another similar jump in evolution. For these new technical developments almost necessarily force all mankind to communicate and to interact more and more strongly, to become more and more closely knit together, whether we like it or not. This is producing great new problems and great new national and international stresses. These stresses may yet kill us. But if we have the sense and the will to solve these problems and to learn how to survive together over the next few years, it seems almost inevitable that we will move toward some wholly new form of human organization and interaction around the world.

We are like men coming out of the dark house of the past into a world of dazzling sunlight. We have climbed up out of the dark cellar where we have been trapped for centuries, isolated, ignorant, selfish, combative, and helpless. Suddenly we find ourselves standing on the threshold of a doorway through which we can see a vista of almost incredible knowledge, abundance, and well-being. If we slam the door in our own faces through our traditional national and international selfishness and clumsiness, we may all go down to nuclear extinction. But if we can work with each other to move successfully together through that doorway, we will find in our hands tremendous new powers and potentialities for the full development of the human spirit and a wholly new ability to shape our own future course. In terms of evolution, it will be a quantum jump. It is what I would like to call, at last, the step to Man.

Let us look at some of our current technical and social changes from this point of view. We can then go on to see what our new scientific developments are telling us about the nature of life and the nature of man as a biological and social and intellectual organism. This will enable us to look more clearly at the possible future or futures of this strange creature, man, and to see how these futures—the possible futures of our own children—might be chosen or shaped or changed into more desirable directions by our choices and actions today.

TECHNOLOGICAL LIMITS

In examining the areas of recent technical change, we find that two features stand out. The first is the fact that the changes today have taken us far beyond the ways of earlier societies. The second is the realization of just how much farther—or how little farther—they may take us in the generations ahead. The changes from the past have been truly enormous. Things are not merely two or three times faster or more powerful than before, but they are changed by many "orders of magnitude"—that is, by many "powers of 10"—so that they go hundreds or thousands or millions of times beyond the ways of previous centuries.

On the other hand, in many areas these vast changes have brought us into a world where the only limits are basic physical or economic limits. In some areas we are near these limits now, in others they are much farther away than we had ever dreamed, but in both cases we are within sight of a kind of "structural maturity" where the techno-social structures, capacities, and rates of flow that mankind develops in the next few decades may represent the structures and limits that will characterize human organization for a very long time to come.

I know that this is a rather surprising conclusion. We are used to the assumption that the rate of change is increasing and that it may go on forever. This may be true in some fields like basic science, biology, and intellectual creation, where there seem to be no physical limits to our growing knowledge. But in more technological areas, when we discover the finiteness of the speed of light, or conversely the almost infinite supply of nuclear energy, we adapt our technology to these facts, and the adaptation may be almost complete within a generation.

Should it surprise anyone that our structures might slow down their rate of change as they reach their natural capacities and limits? Does it surprise us that a boy stops growing physically when he reaches manhood? We have been changing rapidly because we have been passing through an intense and stormy adolescence, and the times may become much calmer as we move toward the structural limits that will determine our future state.

It is easy to show that this is true in one area after another. *Communications.*—Speed of communications is a good example. This has changed incredibly in the last century, but it has now leveled off. The change from the 1800's is a change from the speed of horses and ships, in the range of about 10 miles per hour, to the speed of the telephone, radio, and television, or the speed of light, more than two-thirds of a billion miles per hour. The increase is a factor of more than 10^7, or 10,000,000. But the speed of light is the ultimate limit, since, according to the laws of physics, no matter or energy or signals can ever travel faster than this speed.

The number of communications channels and the coverage of such systems as radio and TV are also approaching limits. Most of the channels are filled, and over half the families in the United States, Russia, and other industrial countries now have telephones, radio, or television, or all three, while the viewing time for TV in American homes now averages several hours per day. Even in the poorer countries the number of television sets is increasing rapidly. Within ten or twenty years, it seems likely that everyone in the world may be hooked into the system for as many hours every single day as his taste or his eyesight can stand.

Communications networks are like the nerves of our worldwide organism. Great improvements in them may still lie ahead, but it is clear that we are no longer very far from the saturation limits that will characterize this kind of human interaction for a long time to come.

Travel.—In the last century, travel speeds have increased from roughly 10 miles an hour by horse and 100 miles an hour by train, to 600 miles an hour by jet plane—with commercial SST planes for about 2,000 miles an hour on the drawing board. This is some two hundred times the speed of horses or ships. For military, business, or personal purposes anywhere in the world, travel time is no longer the most important consideration. Will we go faster? The limit of travel speed in the atmosphere is 17,000 miles an hour if we stay in terrestrial orbit, but men have already done that. It is obvious that human travel over the globe may never be at speeds substantially higher than those already reached.

Even with new kinds of vehicles, it is hard to imagine any device, no matter how remarkable, that would make as great a difference to the structure of our society today as the railroad, the automobile, and the airplane made to the horse-drawn ways of previous centuries. Ours is a mobile society and a jet society. One-fifth of all Americans now move their residence every year. The idea of being attached to a single place becomes quaint and backward—a form of cultural deprivation. Civilians and military personnel are airlifted by the millions overseas and back again every year for the price of two weeks' salary. The custom is spreading to other parts of the population and to other countries as fast as affluence can carry it. The transformation from a static society to a fully mobile society is one that will be substantially complete, at least in the West, within this generation.

Exploration.—In the last twenty years, men have climbed to the top of the highest mountain and have reached the bottom of the deepest ocean. They have lived at stations in the Arctic and

Antarctic all year around with running water and hot showers—
and now with nuclear power. It was only a hundred years ago that
men spent years and risked death to find the source of the Nile.
Today, every square foot of the earth's surface is photographed
daily from orbiting satellites. Many regions need to be studied more
closely, such as the depths of the oceans, but the great age of exploration is evidently over. The earth is finite, and when we have come
to the ends of it, we have come to the ends of it.

Space travel.—The first Sputnik was orbited in 1957. Since
then, many probes have taken close-up pictures of the front side
and the back side of the moon as well as of Venus and Mars. Today
there are hundreds of satellites on various missions flying around
the earth every two hours, and men have already landed on the
moon. These achievements are due to the development of rocket
speeds and rocket capabilities thousands of times beyond anything
in previous centuries.

Yet our capabilities in space may also be within sight of a fundamental plateau. Although many great decades of planetary exploration lie ahead, the time it will take to get to the planets is determined by orbit times, and will not be much shorter than what we
can achieve already. Regardless of what new rockets are devised, it
will probably always take days to get to the moon, months to get to
Venus, Mars, or Mercury, and years or decades to get to Jupiter or
the outer planets.

Computers.—The ENIAC, the first electronic computer, was
built by J. W. Mauchly and J. P. Eckert in 1944. With this device
and its much faster successors, developed along lines suggested by
John von Neumann, the speed of mathematical computation for science or business purposes has increased by about a factor of one
million, or 10^6, over the older "desk calculators" of the 1930s. Calculations in theoretical physics that took a graduate student two
years to finish may now take less than one minute. But some limit
in speeds may now be in sight. This is because the signals cannot
travel between the parts of a computer faster than the velocity of
light. To perform each addition-operation in much less than 10^{-9}
second, or one billionth of a second—about ten times faster than
presently attainable speeds—would require the whole computer to
be much less than a foot in diameter, since this is the distance light
travels in this time. Such a reduction of size is possible with "mi-
cro-miniaturization" of all the computer components, but the costs
rise steeply and will probably set limits on speed that are no longer
very far off.

It should be emphasized, however, that the computer field is one where there are complex possibilities not represented by simple measures of speed. Electronic computers are already taking over many operations in science, industry, and government. These include data processing, calculation, bookkeeping, and management problems. But present studies show that they may also have vast new fields of application to programmed instruction in schools, to pattern perception and language translation, and perhaps, in the next twenty or thirty years, to the complete storage and easy retrieval of all the information in all the books in all the libraries of the world. In their application to intellectual work, computers will be essentially tools and extensions of the human brain and its information-processing capabilities, with applications that can go on growing indefinitely as far as we can foresee.

Cost of research.—Each scientific device or method has its natural limits, but in any area of technological invention and application there may still be "leapfrogging" beyond these limits as entirely new types of discoveries or inventions are made or as whole new areas of science are opened up.

On the other hand, there is a fundamental limit to the total level of support for research and development—R and D. This is an economic limit which may have been nearly reached already in the United States. From 1940 to 1966, federal support for R and D increased two hundred times. From 1950 to 1967, the budget of the National Institutes of Health alone increased almost one hundred times. But in the United States in 1969, the total spent on R and D was about $25 billion, about 3 percent of the gross national product, and the federal government supplied about $16 billion of this. Britain and the Netherlands are now spending more than 2 percent of their national income on R and D. Although it is now obvious how important such a level of spending is for the technical and economic growth and health of a country, it is clear that R and D expenditures are not likely to rise by more than another factor of 2 or so, and that in fact they have already begun to level off because of severe competition from other needs and priorities in our society.

Power.—Two hundred years ago, men changed from animal power to coal power and started the industrial revolution. In 1942 Enrico Fermi and his co-workers made the first atomic or nuclear pile. In 1967 almost half the new electric plants ordered in the United States were nuclear-powered, and it is estimated by some that within a few years large-scale nuclear fission power may become only one-half to one-fifth as expensive as other forms of energy. The uranium and thorium reserves today are estimated to be enough for the power needs of mankind for roughly a million years, offering something like a thousand times more than the energy estimated to be available in coal reserves before nuclear power came along.

This is a case where our breakthrough today is into a world of unbelievable abundance, especially if controlled nuclear "fusion power" can also be developed. Hundreds of millions of dollars are being put into research and development on this question. If success is achieved, it means we can use the almost inexhaustible hydrogen in the oceans for power. This would be an even cleaner and cheaper source than uranium and thorium energy and one available to almost every country. But even without this alternative, it is clear that the step from penury to abundance in energy is one that will be taken all over the world in this generation.

Resources.—What about our other resources—minerals, water, and food? It now appears that we will never run out of minerals. The geochemist Harrison Brown has recently shown that a ton of granite rock contains enough uranium and thorium in trace amounts to equal the energy of several tons of coal. This is enough energy to concentrate all the "trace elements" or minerals in the rock and still have power left over, so that "mining the mountains" in this way can provide all the minerals men will ever need.

In the case of water, our problem today is not one of true shortages but only of wasteful use and pollution. Eventually, with enough energy, we will purify and recycle all the water we use—as the rain purifies and recycles it now. Already, desalination of ocean water with nuclear energy plants has been started, and it promises to provide abundant water in coastal regions all over the world at fairly economical prices.

In the case of food resources, however, the picture is very different. Improved seeds and fertilizers have increased productivity in the last century, but not by an order of magnitude, although there has been a great increase in the human efficiency of farming. In many countries, population has been increasing faster than food, and disastrous famines occur almost every year. If we "farmed the oceans" or if we used nuclear energy to manufacture proteins from coal, the earth might support ten or twenty times the present number of people—or might give the present level of population an undreamed-of-abundance—but there is no evidence that men are adequately pursuing such novel sources. We are evidently within sight of "the time of famines" in which food or inertia—or both—will set the limit on population growth and size, or where alternatively we will learn to control population at some lower level where it will not be limited by the food supply.

Evolution of plants and animals.—It is not generally realized that in this century we have essentially reached the end of the era of evolution of plants and animals by natural selection. It is an era which has lasted some three billion years, during which all the forms of life on earth have proliferated. But today evolution by natural selection is giving way to evolution by human selection. The population of every species on the globe is increasingly determined, accidentally or intentionally, by human breeding, protection, predation, or pollution. The wild animals are being systematically killed, until it is estimated that less than three thousand tigers are now left and less than two thousand of the great whales. There are fairly successful efforts at total extermination of certain bacteria and their insect carriers over wide areas. Our wastes and chemical poisons spread through the air and oceans, affecting animals far from human settlements. On the other hand, we are continually breeding new types of food plants and animals, and even new types of fungi to make penicillin and other drugs.

Undoubtedly the speciation of plants and animals will continue, and the varieties may even become more varied and numerous than in the past—perhaps including the varieties of men!—but they will increasingly be varieties and species that we have allowed to live or that we are breeding deliberately. In the new age, evolution by accident will increasingly be replaced by evolution by human choice.

Disease.—In medicine, the last century also marks the step to the Pasteurian attitude that the causes of diseases can be found and remedied. This is part of the reason why we can control evolution, and why we want to control it. Thousands of disease-causing organisms are now known. Where the necessary public-health measures have been taken, infant mortality has dropped by an order of magnitude, and the average length of life has changed from around thirty years to seventy years or more. In just the last two decades, four of the most serious remaining diseases from bacteria and viruses have been almost conquered—tuberculosis by isoniazid, syphilis by penicillin, malaria by mosquito control with DDT, and infantile paralysis by vaccines and killed virus. A chemical cure for the widespread tropical disease bilharzia, or schistosomiasis, has also been reported.

The result is that in advanced countries the main causes of death are now disorders of cellular function or control—heart disease, brain strokes, and cancer. It is not certain that these can be prevented—indeed there will always be some cause of death!—but massive efforts are being made, and it seems certain that we will never again go back to the pre-Pasteurian attitude of fear, superstition, and helplessness toward disease.

Population growth.—The trouble is that while this marvelous control of disease in the last century has decreased our death rates, birth rates have not come down nearly as fast. As a result, world population has now shot up to more than three billion people, and the doubling time is now between thirty and forty years. In paleolithic times it is estimated to have been about thirty thousand years; so that our rate of increase is now about one thousand times greater than it was for prehistoric man.

Obviously such a rate of increase cannot continue indefinitely. A doubling in 40 years means a fourfold increase in 80 years, eightfold in 120 years, and tenfold in 130 years. This would mean an increase from three billion people to thirty billion people by the year 2100, and to three hundred billion people by the year 2230—that is, in a time shorter than the time since the settling of New England. Yet this number would be far beyond the most optimistic estimates of what the world's food supply could support, even with the use of marginal land and farming the oceans. This consideration is quite aside from the question of whether life at one hundred times our present population density could still be called human. Such a level of crowding is no longer an affirmation of life but a denial of all that life might be.

We see that the population of the planet, like the weight of a grown man, must sometime soon begin to level off to a "steady state," whether this is at some upper limit set by starvation, or at the low limit that would be set by nuclear annihilation, or at some intermediate level of well-being and decency set by sensible human choice. Some day all men will see that an excessively gross population is like an excessively obese man and shows a lack of control that damages its own humanity and its own potentialities.

But is control of population possible? The answer is "yes." The oral contraceptive pill and the intrauterine coil and other promising drug and hormone methods of contraception make the problem look orders of magnitude easier than it did even ten years ago. Millions of women are taking "the pill." The birth rate is dropping rapidly in the United States, and the population already seems to have leveled off in Japan. If birth control can come to be treated as a public health problem, like the control of disease, rather than an individual problem, we might achieve even within this generation the conscious worldwide control of population that all mankind must eventually have for the sake of its health and welfare.

Nuclear weapons.—Turning finally from the technology of life to our most crucial problem today, the worldwide technology of death, we see that the power of bombs and weapons has increased fantastically in the last twenty-five years but has already reached a plateau. In 1944 the greatest bombs were "blockbusters" with about 20 tons of TNT. In 1945 the atomic bombs used on Hiroshima and Nagasaki had a power equivalent to 20,000 tons of TNT. In 1953, with the first explosion of a hydrogen or fusion bomb, the power increased to 20 million tons, or 20 megatons, and the Russians later tested a hydrogen bomb of about 100 million tons. This was an increase in power by a factor of over one million, or 10^6, in ten years. But while it is not technically impossible for the power of bombs to increase further, even militarily it would be a waste of material, since at this level of destruction ten small bombs can destroy a larger area and can be more "effective" than one large bomb.

We have also reached a kind of plateau in the area of "overkill," since both the Russians and the Americans now have enough megatons of nuclear weapons in their arsenals to destroy not only themselves but all life on the planet several times over—with the equivalent of more than 10 tons of explosive for every man, woman, and child alive today, as John F. Kennedy once put it. How can we worry more? The worst is already here.

Control of nuclear weapons.—Yet this means that we may also be near a great step in the control of nuclear weapons and the reduction of terror, simply because the present situation cannot continue. Every year or two now there is some major international confrontation of the nuclear powers—Korea, Berlin, Suez, Laos, Cuba, Vietnam, Israel, last month's crisis, whatever it was—where there is a danger of nuclear threats, nuclear accident, and nuclear escalation. B-52's with hydrogen bombs are still ready to cruise the skies, and Polaris missile submarines hide in the seas. Even though men have worked very hard in each of these crises to avoid disaster, there is always a risk of misunderstood orders or accident, or a dictator ready to commit suicide and pull the world down with him. It is a kind of "nuclear roulette," like spinning the chamber of a revolver with one bullet in it, putting it to your head, and pulling the trigger. Even if you escape the first time, or the second, or the third, it finally, certainly, kills you. If the probability of being killed is only 10 percent each time, it adds to more than 50 percent in a few trials.

Then why do I say we are near a limit in the control of nuclear weapons? Simply because no one lives very long under these conditions. Either in ten or twenty years, or in thirty or forty, we will have fallen over the edge of the precipice, or else we will have found some way to pull back from it by collective agreement or collective rationality of some kind, so that the dangers will be very considerably less, and the world will have some chance of continuing, perhaps, for one hundred or two hundred years. This might give us time to work out still better safeguards to keep from threatening and killing each other, so that we might begin to hope for survival of the human race for two thousand years, or twenty thousand years, say as long as the time since agriculture.

This is not a particularly cheerful view. It sees the human race today as confronted with a very short half-life and with an inescapable choice of whether to go on in the old proud dangerous ways or yield enough to organize internationally for survival. The point is that it is this generation that is the time of choice. The decision of whether we live or die forever will be determined by the efforts of men in the next few years.

In this aspect, then, as in all the other aspects, the present generation is the hinge of history. We see that if we can survive for the next twenty or thirty years, we can move into a high-technology world society reaching across the solar system, with new levels of well-being and hope and fulfillment—a society that might find out how to keep itself alive and evolving for thousands or millions or billions of years. This "step to Man" will be a transition to a new stage in biological and social and intellectual evolution. But the time for the decision is now.

THE DEVELOPMENT OF MAN

How have we come to this place? By tools and fire and speech. Man made them, and then they made man. The invention of tools some two million years ago, according to the findings of L. S. B. Leakey in his Olduvai Gorge excavations, may have led to several of our biological changes, including right-handedness and the development of opposed thumbs useful for grasping. The concentration of attention on making tools and handling fire, especially to solve the problems of survival in cold and marginal habitats during the last Ice Ages, undoubtedly led to an increase in man's cunning and problem-solving abilities and in the size and complexity of his brain, especially in the visual area. Similarly, the invention of speech, with its great power for reporting and analysis, may have led to the survival of men with progressively larger speech areas in the brain.

Fire may have played a major role in the development of our cultural characteristics, as it prolonged the day into long idle evenings when a group could sit around the fire telling stories. The effect of this on the development of speech, symbolism, and systematic language, and on the new inventions of poetry, song, myth, and history, and the systematic teaching of skills, arts, and cultural transmission, must have been enormous.

This learning situation around the fire may also have helped to lengthen our childhood. The great apes are fully adult by the time they are six years old, and perhaps the early men were, too. But man's prolongation of childhood permits an increased duration of protection and teaching by the family which has considerable survival value. The brother or sister who married at age six to live separately in the woods was probably handicapped relative to the ones who matured later and had another year or two at home to practise with fire-tools and arrowheads and making clothes. Obviously, in such a protective teaching system, the parents of a baby have to live long enough for the baby to reach puberty himself, so it may be no accident that the age of puberty today, at about twelve or thirteen for the well-fed, is about half the mean length of life of about twenty-eight years which was characteristic of most of the world until this century.

Are such changes still going on as fast as ever? This is hard to prove, but it seems likely. A threefold increase in brain size in the last two million years would mean only about a one percent increase in the last twenty thousand years, which is too small to measure archeologically with accuracy. But when Julian Huxley listed "the six greatest biological inventions"—clothes, the domestication of plants, the domestication of animals, the fermentation of alcohol, the control of disease, and artificial contraceptives—he noted that the first four were prehistoric, dating from at least twenty thousand years ago. It is hard to believe that these inventions, ushering in stable farms and towns and non-portable wealth, have not changed man as they have changed his plants and animals. And the changes continue. The last two of these inventions were made in the last century, and they have already affected biology enormously.

In fact, Western men have increased in stature by several inches in the last few centuries and by one or two inches in the last generation. Most of us are now too large to fit into the fourteenth-century suits of armor in the museums. This is supposed to be the result of reduced childhood disease and better diets. It would be remarkable if these physical changes in our era were not accompanied by corresponding changes in brain growth and capacity as well.

A further increase in the length of childhood may also be in the offing. Everywhere today the advantage of delayed marriage in terms of family economics and ability to provide for the children is easy to see. In the slums, early childbearing is partly responsible for the high death rate, while in the upper classes marriage is often delayed into the twenties to permit advanced education and advanced earning power. With the average length of life increasing to over seventy, might puberty come to be delayed among intellectuals until their thirties? It is amusing to reflect that many of our geniuses "act as though they had never grown up." It reminds one of how immature a human child would seem among the six-year-old adult chimpanzees.

The inventions today that are the successors to the invention of fire are the use of coal and steam power, electric power, and now atomic power. As the successors to tools, today we have a factory system and great corporations multiplying tools, goods, and weapons and making them cheap and available everywhere. As the successors to speech, we have printed books, movies, and television, multiplying knowledge, communication, and empathy a billionfold around the world. In the long run, these will undoubtedly make as great changes in human biology and organization as fire and tools and speech made two million years ago.

It is only recently that we have been able to look back into the past scientifically to make such comparisons. But now we can open successive doors onto a larger and larger vista of time and space. Our own developments can be put in a broader perspective by observing that the whole evolution of life has been a kind of exercise in problem-solving by ever more sophisticated organisms.

Three methods of problem-solving have now been developed. The first is problem-solving by survival. This is the method of the insects and the lower animals, where the individual organisms are genetically "preprogrammed" or predetermined in their behavior and are unable to learn anything or to change their behavioral patterns during their individual lifetimes. Collectively, however, the species as a whole can "learn," because the individuals that survive and pass their heritage on to their descendants—the gray moths on the tree trunk, say, rather than those that stand out because they are too white or black—are those that embody in their chromosomes and their heredity the genetic variations that are necessary to "solve" their problems and survive.

The second method of problem-solving is problem-solving by individual learning. This came with the development of nervous systems and brains, enabling the individual organism to solve problems by confronting danger and experience short of death. A learning animal could draw back from the cliff before he fell over and could look ahead and behind and associate things of value to survival.

The first of these problem-solving methods is "phylogenetic"—problem-solving by the species as a whole. The second is "ontogenetic"—problem-solving by the individual. In the last few hundred years we have acquired a third method, problem-solving by anticipation; that is, by science—by analysis and prediction. Rudiments of this method have been with us since the invention of language and thought, but today it has become the most powerful tool of civilized man. It is a method which can solve problems in advance, often before they happen, and sometimes even before they have ever happened to anyone. And occasionally, what is most difficult of all, it can solve problems even while they are in progress, with feedback loops and "cybernetic" control mechanisms or goal-directed mechanisms.

Thus when the first Sputnik was sent up, it did not just happen to go into the proper path because it was the only one of thousands of Sputniks that survived. And it did not try a high path and then a low one, learning by trial which one was too fast or too slow. Problem-solving by survival or by trial-and-error learning would have been too wasteful. No: the Sputnik went into the correct orbit on the first try because the development of science had enabled the laws of physics to be discovered, which permitted the calculation of the trajectory in advance and the construction of a feedback control-system to steer in the chosen direction and to turn off the rocket motors at the right time to reach the preset path.

The methods of problem-solving are thus by survival, which emphasizes the accidental heritage of past individuals; by learning, which emphasizes the present individual and his experience; and by anticipation, which emphasizes the planned shaping of the future. That is, by the species; by the individual; and then by science. Or we could say that they are by the DNA, the hereditary material in the chromosomes of the cells; by the neurons, the connected cells of the brain; and then by computers and cybernetic process-control programs, the artificial electronic networks that our brains have set up. As the DNA created the cells of the brain, so the brain has now created equations and computers to solve them.

We have now stepped up onto the third step of this evolutionary progression. If we are skillful and wise, it is now possible to anticipate and to shape physical, biological, and social futures which have never existed before; and to seize golden opportunities; and to solve deadly problems sometimes even before we come to them.

It is fortunate that this is so, because we have indeed come into a world of new opportunities and of new and deadly problems such as have never existed before. They cannot be solved by any other method than by scientific analysis and anticipation, and they will almost certainly destroy us if we wait to learn how to solve them in the old way by living through them.

We can see the main reason for our new difficulties if we utilize "general systems theory," which deals with the analogies and differences between living systems at different levels of organization, such as a cell, an organism, a family, an industrial organization, or a nation. These are all fairly well-integrated systems which develop, so to speak, from within, and which have integrative feedbacks or decision structures that tend to prevent any great destructive tension between the component parts throughout all the stages of growth.

The trouble is that the world today is not a development of this kind but something more like an intersection of competing systems. The groups and nations that are colliding today have not been developed as parts of an integrated organism with a single tested set of genetic instructions for relating the parts, or with established decision rules. Consequently, the pressures and conflicts between them have no counterpart in the growth of an organism, and the question is whether adequate protective interactions and decision rules can be adopted before the tension destroys the whole undertaking. Possibly our new understanding of systems organization, and of social and political problem-solving by anticipation, can be translated into a workable solution in time, but the time is short.

This moment of decision has arrived with startling suddenness on the evolutionary scale. This can be seen by repeating a comparison which Julian Huxley first made, between the history of life and the height of St. Paul's Cathedral. If the three billion years or so of life are represented by the height of the Cathedral, which is more than 300 feet, each foot represents roughly ten million years. The two million years of man is about the height of a 2-inch block lying on top of the roof. The twenty thousand years since agriculture began is about the thickness of a postage stamp on top of the block. The four hundred years of modern science and industry is the thickness of the ink on the postage stamp. And the thirty to fifty years from the coming of atomic energy and television and space travel to the time when we must make a more stable organization of the world, or perish, is only the thickness of the film of moisture on top of the ink.

This almost instantaneous step to a viable human organization for survival, this step to Man, is essentially the creation of a new species and a new world. If we can manage to keep from killing ourselves as we set up these new structures, it will make us participants in the most incredible event in evolution, as the Jesuit philosopher Teilhard de Chardin emphasized. This step differs—in its suddenness, its global character, its biological control, its order-of-magnitude changes, and its requirements for conscious planning—from everything that has gone before. All of evolution up to now has been but prologue.

THE RANGE OF LIFE

Life may not be nearly as unusual as it was thought to be in the nineteenth century. Hydrogen, carbon, nitrogen, and oxygen—the chemical elements necessary for life as we know it—are the most abundant combining elements in the universe. The astronomers are now saying that when a star, or sun, condenses out of the dust clouds in interstellar space and begins to be self-luminous from the nuclear reactions in it, some of the remaining dust may condense around it into planets. In the flux of radiation from the sun, the chemical elements on the surface of a planet can form more and more complex molecules. The picture of how these might build up to life was developed by A. I. Oparin in the 1930's. Later, Harold Urey and Stanley Miller showed experimentally that a simple electric discharge, through a mixture of small molecules like methane, ammonia, and water, produced many of the amino acids which are the building blocks of proteins in living cells. Even more complex molecules, such as the nucleic acids and porphyrin, which is the basis of the chlorophyll in green plants, have now been made by such methods. The same result could be obtained by ultraviolet radiation from the sun, although more slowly.

Oily hydrocarbons have now been found in meteorites, and the question is being studied whether they have been formed in this pre-biological way or whether they are of biological origin. Either possibility would be extremely interesting. The findings of complex molecules on the surfaces of the moon and Mars is still possible.

Very complex molecules are still, of course, a long way from the self-reproducing or "self-catalytic" processes that are necessary to life. Many experimental and theoretical studies are under way to see how this gap could have been bridged and whether it takes a billion years of sunlight under conditions on the primitive earth or can be bridged more quickly today in the laboratory. Some bacteria-like structures have recently been found in rocks 3.0 billion years old, but it seems certain that there must have been pre-cellular stages that go back much closer to the origin of the earth 4.5 billion years ago, although concrete evidence for such stages may be hard to find.

Some have speculated that life elsewhere, at different temperatures and pressures, might involve "exotic chemistry," such as the use of ammonia in place of water, or silicon chains in place of carbon, but the possible compounds and reactions in such systems now appear to be rather limited. On the other hand, life as we know it survives over an astonishing range of conditions. Viruses and bacteria can survive long exposures to vacuum and to temperatures near absolute zero. Algae and bacteria live from below the freezing point to near the boiling point of water, and worms and arthropods are even found at pressures of 1,000 atmospheres at the bottom of the Pacific. The search for living systems, perhaps at the poles of Venus or in hot springs on Mars, or perhaps at the warm bottoms of the cold atmospheres of the outer planets like Jupiter and Saturn, now seems quite reasonable to many chemists and biologists and is one of the most interesting aspects of the space program.

The basic chemical elements are the same everywhere. Should it surprise us if the functional and self-reproducing organic compounds and combinations also turn out to be the same everywhere? We are made of the dust of the universe, and it may be more familiar than we have been willing to admit.

Even the shapes of creatures elsewhere might not be so different from ours. The shapes of organisms tend to fit the symmetry of their mode of life. Organisms floating in water tend to be round. But swimmers and burrowers that have a directed motion have a head and a tail; and the sensory organs, the nose and eyes and the mouth, are all at the head end where they encounter new environments first. Crawlers over a surface have a belly and a back, with the back more heavily protected. Flyers, whether birds or bats, all have rather similar wings to beat the air.

This is "convergent evolution," and the explanation for it is that there are only certain ways to solve certain problems, no matter where you start from. Will the Martians or the creatures from Alpha Centauri look like us, as the science-fiction movies suggest? This general systems theory suggests that the answer is probably "yes." We know many varieties of solutions to the problem of life, from the slime mold to the Sequoia, and from the ladybug to the peacock and the whale, but they fit within these general regularities, and it is therefore hard to imagine any forms of organic life elsewhere that could be much more bizarre than things we have seen already.

Will there be higher forms of life elsewhere that can communicate with us? No one knows, but there is no reason to believe that evolution in some other places may not be just as advanced as ours or even far ahead. The trouble is that our galaxy, the Milky Way, is so vast that even if it contained millions of such centers of life, the nearest one might still be hundreds of light-years away. But such questions are no longer far from the minds of modern astronomers, as Iosif Shklovskiy and Carl Sagan have emphasized. Radio astronomers have recently searched for signal-like emissions at various wavelengths. They are intrigued by some peculiar OH-molecule emissions that suggest some kind of high-intensity "laser" sources, and more recently by the discovery of those "pulsar" sources in the sky giving highly regular bursts of radio energy periodically every second or so. Space beacons, or new types of neutron stars? Whatever they are, we may be the galactic babies who are just about to realize that the parents are saying words. But, of course, any intelligent beings elsewhere might have methods of high-intensity communication that are still hundreds or thousands of years beyond any technology that we can detect or understand today.

All this suggests that even the process of evolution itself should be looked at from a larger point of view. Joshua Lederberg has divided the possible evolutionary processes into three sequential stages, which he calls "chemogeny," "biogeny," and "cognogeny." The stage of chemogeny would be the early stage of preorganic evolution of complex molecules in a star's radiation field. Biogeny would begin when the abundance of different molecules begins to be dominated by self-amplifying processes, with natural selection. On the earth this stage would include all of our evolution, from the one-celled and the many-celled plants and animals up until the appearance of man.

The era of cognogeny in any evolutionary system would begin

with symbolic and technical understanding and manipulation. That is, it would begin on earth with the coming of human speech, brains, and scientific control, as man begins to dominate the world and its plants and animals and to shape the course of evolution deliberately. On an evolutionary time-scale, we are still on the uncertain threshold of this era.

It is interesting to realize that the "creatures" of the cognogenic era no longer need to be limited to biological cells and protoplasm. The astronomer Fred Hoyle suggested in *The Black Cloud* that the sensory-motor networks of a higher organism might be organized into a huge dust cloud in space, with radio waves for nerve signals and magnetic fields for muscles. We would not know how to create such a vast system, but we do know how to create increasingly sophisticated automatic systems, sensory-motor decision-systems or "cybernetic organisms," on our own scale.

The Surveyor landing devices that started photographing and digging up and analyzing the surface of the moon and sending back information before the manned landings in 1969 are automata of this kind. Exploratory development has also been started on a larger "Automated Biological Laboratory," or ABL, for exploring the surface of Mars in an even more sophisticated way. This would be a large vehicle with wheels, a nuclear power source, and microwave communication back to earth. It would contain telescopes, microscopes, manipulators, and a complete analytical laboratory directed by its own computer. It would be stabilized so it could move over the landscape to dig up samples, and the hope is that it would then be able to make automatically any analysis or microbiological study that can be done today in a terrestrial laboratory. In fact, the cost of developing such a device might pay off handsomely, not only in the development of automata for hazardous work, but also in showing how to automate our own biochemical laboratories.

The value of the ABL concept is in the flexibility and "intelligence" of the device. It would be orders of magnitude more valuable than a pre-programmed system because it could change its analyses with new information, and it could be re-programmed to do new experiments and answer new questions that are not thought of until months or years after it had been sent off on its mission.

What would an ABL look like to a Martian? Like some kind of jointed, animate creature, with internal energy, arms, eyes, ears, strange feeding habits, and peculiar but directed behavior. Although it could not yet reproduce itself, it is no longer impossible for us to see how to program such a creature to do so. (On earth, it would only have to type out orders to various factories for all of its component parts and fit them together in assembly jigs when they arrived.)

The age of cognogeny has taken us beyond neural networks to a worldwide communications network of knowledge. We see that it is also taking us beyond the age of protoplasm to the age of electronic automata which will handle more and more of the work and science of the world. As our biological cells long ago began to "secrete" and assemble our own neural networks, so we now have begun to secrete automated systems, their designers, slaves, and masters. It may be another case of convergent evolution, happening everywhere in the universe.

SHAPING OUR PSYCHOLOGY

One of the most important discoveries in psychology in the twentieth century is "operant conditioning." This remarkable and powerful behavioral method is linked with the name of B. F. Skinner and goes far beyond the older associative conditioning of Pavlov. Pavlov showed that a dog, having learned to associate the sound of a bell with food, would eventually salivate at the sound of the bell alone. Skinner showed, on the other hand, that an animal could learn to do much more and could master a very complex task, if he were given an immediate reward or "reinforcement" for every small step along the way. A pigeon or a dog, for example, might be given a morsel of food, or even just a "secondary reinforcer," such as a clicking sound that has been associated with food, every time he comes closer to performing a given task. In this way a dog can be quickly taught to open a cupboard door, and a pigeon can be taught to stand on tiptoes or to play table tennis. It is called "operant conditioning" because the animal himself does the operating which the experimenter reinforces. With the instant reward or feedback, he can sometimes learn in a few minutes what took days or weeks of trial-and-error learning by the older teaching methods.

Skinner suggests that for a baby the primary reinforcement is the mother's milk and comfort, and the secondary reinforcers are the attention of the eyes, the expression, and tone of voice. These reinforcers, repeated by the rest of the family and friends, are powerful feedbacks that shape our behavior for the rest of our lives.

It is noteworthy that Skinner finds that punishment—or "aversive reinforcement"—always damages the rate of learning of a task. Simply turning off the reinforcement after a wrong response is far more effective in quickly eliciting the right response than any shock or physical blow. We suddenly realize that punishment has been used throughout history, not because it speeds up the child's learning, but because it is a simple quick response which is "reinforcing" for the teacher.

The power of the Skinner method of teaching comes from three things: its speed, its transfer to secondary reinforcers, and the use of random or probabilistic reinforcement. After a few rewards have been given, and a task has been learned, an animal will go on repeating the same behavior even when the reinforcements are given only occasionally. The behavior may become even "stronger" and more compulsive if the reinforcement is given at random, say one time in five or ten or fifty, as in the payoff from a slot machine. This gives us for the first time an explanation of the addictive character of gambling, which has been very hard to explain in terms of the traditional list of psychological motivations and biological needs. With random reinforcement, birds or rats will press a bar thousands of times an hour for the occasional reward and will go on for hours, like Las Vegas gamblers, even when the effort costs them far more than they get back. These fast responses are now being used by psychologists to obtain data on animal perception and discrimination far more rapidly and accurately than has ever been possible before.

Teaching and learning.—Operant conditioning is also the basis of the Skinner "teaching machines" or what is called more generally "programmed instruction." In the teaching machines or the new "teaching books," the material to be learned is broken into small successive bits, and these bits are set down in sequence on a lesson sheet or on the page of the book. The student puts his answer or an "x" in a space and then uncovers a comparison answer to get an immediate feedback as to whether he is right, before going on to the next question. The success of the method depends critically on the skillful design of the program, but a spelling lesson or a physics lesson may be broken into twenty or thirty points, and a student may master these, with several repetitions, in less time than it takes to get across the same points in a lecture. This permits each student to progress at his own rate, and it saves enormously on teacher time.

More complex versions of this kind of instruction are now being programmed into computers. The sequence of instruction materials or questions is presented on the face of a picture tube, and the student can reply by typing out answers or questions on an electric typewriter or by using a "light pen" to point to answers on the face of the tube, again with instant reinforcement for correct answers. There is special emphasis on flexible "branching programs," where the kind of answer a student makes determines whether the next step will be easy or hard. It now appears that complete courses such as college algebra can be programmed in this way, so that the classroom teacher may be able to get away from elementary or repetitious material and spend more time on the larger aspects of the subject.

Of course, similar reinforcement methods are used by a human parent or teacher, reinforcing with the eyes or a nod of approval, as teachers always have, or reinforcing more formally by awarding "points" to the pupils at random when they are behaving or answering properly. These points may be translated later into more tangible rewards such as privileges or food, just as they always have been in families giving love and approval to their children's behavior. It is said that these formal reinforcement methods are much more effective than traditional teacher behavior in generating an enthusiasm for learning, even with "problem children."

It is becoming clear that programmed instruction of various kinds may have as great an impact on mass education and self-education as the invention of printed books had five hundred years ago. It may be the only way in which we can transmit our complex high-technology culture to the hundreds of millions of children around the world who need it not only for personal development but also for the development of their nations.

Studies of "early enrichment" are making another kind of revolution in education. It has now been proved that rich sensory experience in infancy is necessary for the development of the higher nervous system. Deprivation of companionship leads to bizarre adult behavior, and David Krech and others have shown that animals kept in a deprived or dull environment have poor problem-solving abilities, while animals from the same litter kept in an enriched environment grow up with much more intelligence.

This has led to a massive reexamination of our assumptions about the development of intelligence in human children. It now appears that cultural enrichment between ages one and four can raise a child's intelligence quotient, or I.Q., by about ten points, and enrichment between the ages of four and sixteen can raise it by another ten points. The low I.Q.'s of slum children, which are often near 80 instead of the normal 100, may result not from their genetics, as is often supposed, but from their cultural poverty, and may be raised to the normal level by early tutoring programs as well as by better nutrition before and after birth.

Still worse difficulties may be produced by the actual anti-educational attitudes of parents in many cultures and subcultures. It is found that they may often suppress imaginative play, for example, because it is "unreal" or "may lead to telling lies." Since imagination is the basis for abstraction and for symbolizing one object by another, children from such cultures may have serious difficulties when they get into school in reading and in learning what letters and words mean. Fortunately it is known that a few minutes a day is enough to get a young child started on imaginative play and symbolization. Thus a change in parental attitudes could greatly affect education in the next generation.

Other innovations in curriculum and teaching methods from kindergarten through high school, in science, mathematics, and many other subjects, are making a new educational revolution in the United States today. Education is becoming more concrete, more personal, and more interesting at all levels, and the difference can already be seen in the brilliance and enthusiasm of the students. It is not certain what the genetic limits are on human intelligence and problem-solving abilities, but it now appears that we have never been educating children anywhere close to them. With these new educational ideas and methods, the average child may be able to reach intellectual achievements far beyond what we had ever dreamed. The extension of these improvements to all schools and all countries will make an enormous difference in the quality of life in the world in the decades ahead.

COLLECTIVE SELF-DETERMINATION

The possibility of shaping our collective future in the directions we want to go depends on the wise application of these new and powerful tools. This is an organizational problem, and a problem in the politics of self-interested human interactions. The issue is as follows. As we have seen, self-predictions of our conscious choices are not real predictions in the noninterfering sense like predicting rain— which is the only sense in which we can speak of determinism. By the same token, predictions of the behavior of a decision-system are not predictions but persuasions communicated to the system. With full interpersonal communication, a decision-system such as a person or an integrated social group ceases to be an "object" and becomes a "co-subject," with all the subjective and goal-directed freedom of choice that that implies. It is not a "thou" but an "I-thou," as Buber would say.

From our discussion earlier, this means that our whole society is in principle unpredictable as a deterministic object, except perhaps statistically, because interpersonal communication is precisely the basis on which a society is constructed. Society is capable of changing to a new course at any time because of some objectively unforeseeable individual act of insight or decision within a single brain— some act of leadership or violence or invention—that carries the whole society along with it.

This conclusion goes considerably beyond the concept of cybernetics, as developed by Norbert Wiener; that is, the concept of feedback which can guide goal-directed behavior in animate or inanimate systems. Cybernetics has been one of the great seminal ideas of the mid-twentieth century. It is the basic principle of teleological behavior, or action with "purpose," and therefore it is one of the important ways in which biology goes far beyond physics and chemistry. Goal-directed feedback is our way of understanding the biological phenomenon of "homeostasis," or stabilization responses, which Walter Cannon emphasized, as well as the more important phenomenon of internally directed growth. As Albert Szent-Gyorgyi has put it,

> Life is not like physical things . . . If you use your car a lot, the car wears out and your legs get weak, but if you walk a lot, your legs get strong. The non-living wears itself out by work; but the living builds itself up.

Such ideas make Aristotle's discussion of purpose in natural systems seem much more scientific and less objectionable than they seemed to the nineteenth-century determinists.

And what we are seeing here is that these cybernetic ideas can now be extended, as we conceive of the brain not as a simple feedback loop or directed growth pattern, but as a "parallel-processing decision-system stabilized with self-reinforcing feedback loops," with properties that go beyond any simple feedback or computer statement of the problem. This larger picture of the mechanisms of perceptual and mental organization has profound implications for our scientific and philosophical understanding not only of the brain but of the relation of an intelligent choosing organism to the environment and the society with which it interacts.

"LOCK-INS" AND SOCIAL STRUCTURE

These ideas of systems and of self-reinforcing loops can thus be applied in a fruitful way to society itself and to the problems of human interactions of cooperation and conflict. One earlier useful application of a systems and feedback approach is shown in the economic theories of John Maynard Keynes, designed to try to stabilize national economic growth.

With the newer ideas, it is also becoming possible now to analyze certain self-reinforcing "lock-in situations" which represent the most dangerous situations in the world today. Lock-ins occur in any ongoing flow system, where the flow itself sets up forces that maintain the existing patterns and keep them from being easily changed. A mechanical example is that of a stick wedged against a rock in a waterfall, which may be held in one position by the force of the water so as to deflect the waterfall to one side and affect its course far down the river, unless the stick can be lifted and moved to another position. The ruts in a country road represent a historical lock-in of successive vehicles into the original track.

In fact, it could be said that all that we mean by "permanence" in a dynamic ongoing world is a self-reinforcing loop or lock-in of some kind at a given level of organization—a reconciliation of Heraclitus with Democritus, of the world of flow with the world of objects. An atom, for example, is made of self-reinforcing "standing waves" of electrons. The enzyme molecules that persist for eons are those that contribute to a self-maintaining system. The wings of birds or bats are locked in to shapes that work, and this kind of self-reinforcement happens whenever we have convergent evolution.

These ideas can be generalized to the case of "multiple lock-ins," in which a set of different "solutions" interact and stabilize each other. A good example is the case of vowel sounds, where the choice of a given vowel sound in a given dialect affects neighboring vowel sounds, almost as though there were a physical repulsion between them. So Americans have the one-syllable words "bee" and "bay" but not "beh"; "he" and "hay" but not "heh"; "see" and "say" but not "seh"; and so on. The child who uses the intermediate sound is corrected, and laughed at, and finally may not get what he wants. These vowel sounds are locked in to each other, so that they may all shift together as we go from one dialect to another or as the spoken language changes over the years. One can see similar relationships of mutual stabilization among the animals in an ecological system, as the lion's characteristics, for example, are locked in to the speed of the antelope and the toughness of the water buffalo.

In social systems, the choice of a left-hand or a right-hand rule for traffic on two-way streets represents a lock-in which is initially arbitrary but which is self-maintaining and has to be universal if accidents are to be avoided. A more subtle example is that of multiple psychological lock-ins between the members of a family, with their roles and relations remaining almost unchanged for years until someone leaves or dies or a new wife is brought in. Great industrial organizations may become locked in on the manufacture of cars or the manufacture of weapons, while other public needs, of equal importance and possibly equal profit in the long run, go begging for a solution.

In national policy, there may be multiple lock-ins between the presidency, the Congress, the opposition party, the newspapers, the military-industrial complex, the voters, and the policies of foreign governments. As a result, the options available to a President or to a congressman running for office may be very narrow, because any change would change the number of his sympathizers or opponents, many of whom are locked in by local forces in their turn.

What mechanisms of change may be available when these lock-ins become destructive of larger human purposes? The problem is difficult but it is not entirely hopeless. One possible mechanism is a change of ideas and standards leading to a drift of the whole system, which is perhaps what brought the civil rights movement to success after World War II. Another is the sudden introduction of new technological devices, as in the case of the long-playing record, which changed the diversity of home music; or the computer, which is changing banking; or nuclear weapons, which have changed the face of war. Another mechanism is the steady changes of technological scale which alter the "space" of the lock-ins or the ecosystem. For example, modern technology and communications have altered the space within which nations move and the speed and complexity of their choices, forcing government by hereditary kings of doubtful ability to be replaced by government by committees of managers.

The lock-ins of habit, custom, and poor organizational design poison the performance of many of our smaller organizations, such as small businesses, schools, public organizations, and cities. As a result, our lives and our work are harder and less pleasant than they could be with the same resources but with a more responsive organizational structure and better handling of new information and change. Technical solutions and rules for restructuring the lock-in problems at this level might give improved payoffs for everyone involved, and might do more than almost anything else to release the creative social energies of our people.

In all these cases, we are able to see the reaction which needs to be catalyzed, so to speak, and we see that the energy change is favorable, but there is an organizational barrier. The problem is to invent a "social enzyme" that will get around it or that will dissolve and restructure these self-maintaining lock-ins. Perhaps with practice and with a body of decision-rules for social cooperation, this process may become easier than it is today.

Conflict and the problem of the "Prisoner's Dilemma."— "Prisoner's Dilemma" is a "game" which simulates a particularly dangerous lock-in conflict situation between competing human beings, and which is now being extensively analyzed for the light it may throw on larger social problems. This game simulates the situation of two prisoners suspected by the police who are kept apart and interrogated and urged to tell on each other. If both cooperate (with each other) and refuse to talk, both may get off lightly in the absence of other evidence. If both "defect" and tell on each other, both are punished. But if only one "defects," he gets a reward, while the one who has continued to cooperate "gets the book thrown at him," with a much more severe sentence.

Under these circumstances, what is the "rational" choice for each man to make? It is clearly to each man's immediate advantage to defect, no matter what the other man does—which is why the police set up such a reward system. Yet if they both defect, they are both worse off than if both had tacitly cooperated with each other by keeping silent. We see that in this case there is a "collective rationality" which differs from "individual rationality" but which would nevertheless have higher payoffs for both individuals. This is not a "zero-sum game" like chess or poker, where one player wins what another loses, but is a "non-zero-sum game" where both players may win or lose together.

Anatol Rapoport and his co-workers have had hundreds of pairs of students play this kind of game over and over again in order to see what the actual behavior of human beings is like in such a dilemma. The players are not allowed to communicate with each other (except through the consequences of their plays), and they receive small monetary rewards or losses which simulate the "rewards" to the prisoners. On repeated plays, the behavior of each pair of students tends to lock in, with both tending to defect on each other all the time, or both tending to cooperate.

Another non-zero-sum game is the game of "Chicken," like the "game" played by teen-agers who drive cars toward each other at high speed down the middle of the road. If one driver "cooperates" by swerving aside, both are saved, but the cooperator loses in prestige because he is "chicken"; if neither swerves, both lose heavily. These and many other non-zero-sum games which exhibit other dilemmas of individual versus collective rationality are now being simulated in the laboratory. Each type of game is found to call forth its own type of threat or sacrifice, of leadership, conflict, or co-operation in the players.

The importance of these games is that they show on a small scale and in a quantitatively measurable way the kind of social behavior that may occur between neighbors in a lawsuit or between nations using nuclear threats and "brinkmanship" against each other. Kenneth Boulding has said, "Prisoner's Dilemma is the fruit-fly of social interaction," meaning that such laboratory gaming may teach us as much about the mechanisms of social conflict and cooperation as fruit fly studies have taught us about genetics in recent years.

In fact, these studies already suggest several important insights into the problems of international conflict, which are our most dangerous world problems today. For one thing, we see that the problems of life and death and the large problems of the world are all non-zero-sum problems. In biology, all the organs of the body are healthy together or sick together. In economics, we all prosper together or suffer depression together. In international nuclear politics, we either live a better life together or die together. It is not true that the life of mankind is some kind of zero-sum poker game where one nation simply wins what the other nation loses. And the familiar strategy of individual rationality and of secrecy and bluffing and defection, which works so well around the poker table, may be disastrous in this different kind of game.

Second, it helps to see that in such games there is a real dilemma between the strategy that is individually rational in the short run and the strategy that will obtain larger payoffs to all individuals when the game keeps going on. This makes it less puzzling that there should be such violent differences on national courses of action between intelligent men who are each trying to do the best thing for the country. It is clear that in such cases communication between the conflicting parties or nations is of great value in making sure of reaching a strategy profitable to both. The locking in of cooperation (or defection) in these dilemma-games also suggests that a series of small steps on which the parties can cooperate initially may greatly increase the probability of cooperative behavior on large steps later.

Third, we see the value of internalized moral rules in dilemma-behavior. Whenever communication or prediction is imperfect, it increases the average payoffs if all the players tend to have some general moral rules or "heuristic rules" suggesting that short-run individual rationality may be very costly to everybody in the long run. The thief keeps the faith with the thieves, is a survival-principle for bands of thieves. Such rules help lock in on the cooperative solution. Moral rules are like rules of speaking in order at a meeting or driving a car on the right-hand side, suggesting social behavior patterns that give us collective benefits in general without having to think each time about what to do.

What is most important about Prisoner's Dilemma, however, is that it sharpens up our understanding of our world danger today by showing that the origin of our danger now is not "primordial evil" of our "unreconstructed lower brain" or some "flaw" in the nature or behavior of man but is rather a lock-in conflict-dilemma between independent social systems. Some recent writers have emphasized the aggressive biological background of mankind, as though this were the whole origin of our problems; and they have spoken of "the Territorial Imperative" of animals and tribes to stake out their own territories and defend them. But if this were the basic trouble with the world, there would be no countries or groups of countries with internal peace and security, such as the Scandinavian countries have, and no countries with undefended borders, such as the U.S.-Canadian border.

No: these defects and hostile drives of individual men are real, but they can be minimized with good educational and social systems and with enough to eat, and they are simply not very relevant to the crisis problems of the world today which are social-structural rather than animalistic. Discussion of such drives may even make the international problems worse by suggesting to many people that these problems are inescapably built into the nature of man and that hence nothing can be done about them. The lethal dangers in the world today are not due to these flaws in individual man but to the fact that independent social systems with nuclear weapons are forced to live together in a shrinking world—"like scorpions in a bottle," as Robert Oppenheimer said—with independent internal dynamics and with hostile and self-aggravating lock-ins that are not coordinated for their real mutual interests.

Make a more unified decision-network for this organism, mankind—a network that will have practical ways of settling differences and of keeping the peace between the parts—and our fears of the total annihilation of biological man will decrease sharply, regardless of all our subconscious aggressions and our territorial imperatives. Man is now created by culture; and a culture adequately structured for intercontrol, intergrowth, and intereducation will produce security, prosperity, well-being, and much more peaceful men. Can it be done? Almost certainly. But it is not certain whether we have enough dedicated men with the vision and skill to lead us to do it within the shrinking time that remains.

DEVELOPMENTS AHEAD

Herman Kahn and his co-workers and Daniel Bell and his colleagues have recently suggested lists of new technical developments that they predict will be made by the year 2000. Most of their items are items from physics and engineering, such as fusion power, the control of weather, and artificial hearts. But it is possible to add to their lists several important developments in biological technology that lie close ahead.

Genetic copying of animals.—As we have seen, each of the cells of an adult organism seems to contain in its nucleus and chromosomes the full information necessary for the development of the whole organism. Michael Fischberg and J. B. Gurdon, using a micropipette, have taken a single cell nucleus from a cell of a developed tadpole and have reimplanted this nucleus into a fertilized frog egg in place of the egg's own nucleus. They have shown that in a good percentage of the cases this egg will then grow into a fully fertile adult frog which is a genetic duplicate of the animal from which the nucleus was taken.

If this method could be extended to higher animals such as chickens, hogs, and cattle, it would give rise to a billion-dollar business. It would make possible the copying of the best animals in each flock or herd, which could give rise to a whole herd of "instant champions" in a single breeding season. This could increase meat, milk, and egg production in many countries by 50 to 100 percent. Plants and some of the lower animals can propagate copies from pieces of themselves, but copying has not been done with vertebrates before, so in a sense this is the most revolutionary development in evolution in the last half-billion years. If this method can be extended to higher animals, the change in our level of control over our biological environment and the implications for human biology in the long run could be very great.

Contraceptives in foods.—There are stories that various primitive tribes may have eaten certain plants with contraceptive properties. The development and use of contraceptives in foods was advocated by Homi Bhabha, late chief of the Indian Atomic Energy Commission. This would greatly simplify the practice of contraception. In fact, many an American community today might gladly vote to replace their daily pills, intra-uterine coils, and other devices by such a convenient method, if it were available and were known to be safe and effective. To adopt such a system would require, of course, a democratic decision by a nation as to whether it should be adopted, and it would require that there be "other stores" where a couple could go to buy untreated food if they really wanted to have children. But this would mean that every child was a wanted child —not necessarily a bad or immoral thing at all for the children of the world!

To be effective, the contraceptive substances would have to be put in widely used processed foodstuffs, such as salt, sugar, bread, rice, or beer, as a public health measure, in the same way that we now put chlorine in water, iodine in salt, and Vitamin D in milk. Finding a contraceptive that can be taken by all ages and sexes without undesirable side effects might be difficult, but it is not necessarily impossible, considering how many different types of contraceptive substances we know.

The important thing about this approach of Bhabha's is that it could result in the beginning of a leveling off of population in the most desperate countries perhaps ten to twenty years sooner— hundreds of millions of babies sooner—than present contraceptive methods requiring individual medical help. This is because the biochemical development, testing, and implementation might require only a few years, if the history of the development of oral contraceptives is any guide; while the problem of reaching hundreds of millions of individuals with present methods would require many years of work by hundreds of thousands of paramedical personnel who have to be trained in training centers that will take many more years to set up and to staff.

The payoff of this kind of positive contraceptive method, with its provision for individual choice—for "wanted" children—would therefore be enormous, in terms of human hope and health and happiness. Just to know that a leveling off of the population explosion is within sight would give us all a new level of hope and confidence and could open up many new economic resources in planning for the future.

Regeneration of organs.—If all the information necessary for the development of a whole organism is present in every adult cell, it should be possible to regenerate a cutoff finger or hand, instead of just being able to grow a little skin over the stump. Lobsters can regenerate claws, and newts can regenerate whole eyes and optic nerves, as we have mentioned. Why not man? Maybe it would take some application of salt solutions, embryonic fluids, tissue inducers extracted from lower animals, or some kind of neural or electrical excitation, since we know that innervation is necessary for muscle growth. But there are many ways to try, and if something like this could be done, many might prefer growing a new finger or hand, even slowly, rather than having to have a clumsy mechanical prosthesis. It is said that less than a dozen biologists are working in this field today. If a few dozen more would volunteer or could be assigned to work on this problem—as they are assigned in military medicine to work on prosthetic devices—the payoff for amputees and persons disfigured in accidents could conceivably be very high.

New channels of personal communication.—As we have seen, speech, words, and language were one of the prehistoric inventions that made men men. But speech comes through a single channel— the throat. Considering the multiple-channel character of the brain, and how much we are beginning to know about parallel processing, communication and information theory, and linguistics, the question arises whether today we might go beyond this primitive invention of speech and find or create a group of additional parallel channels of person-to-person communication. Facial expressions and tone of voice give us some parallel channels, but these channels, while important, are few and not very specific.

One place where additional parallel channels might be acquired is in the fingers. One can imagine a rubber glove fitted, say to the left hand of a small child, with the child taught to manipulate his muscles like a pianist or violinist, so that several electrical contacts in the glove could pick up his muscle signals in a precise way. The hand has nineteen bones with opposed pairs of muscles, and this would give at least nineteen parallel channels, whose signals could then be broadcast from a low-power radio on the child's wrist. A teacher or another child with a similar radio and glove might pick up these signals and have them transformed back into electrical pulses going to, say, nineteen other small electrodes touching the back of the hand in a one-to-one correspondence.

With such a system, one particular flexing of the fingers might convey a graph, another a sketched cartoon, and another might transmit a whole sentence or an explicit pattern of ideas in a single gesture. Speeches that now take an hour might take minutes! Obviously, such a system would require a new language—or more exactly, a new "manuage," since it uses the hand rather than the tongue. New symbols would have to be devised to represent it in print. It might require a new syntax, a syntax of multiple pattern relations, and it might lead away from our present sequential logic to more complex forms of logic and perhaps to new modes of implication and thought.

Would this not be an important project to undertake at this moment when we need so much to understand each other better? Explorations in this direction would be worth working on by a group of the best electrical engineers, communications experts, linguists, psychologists, and child development personnel. Conceivably a few years of intensive effort might produce an invention as revolutionary for personal communication as the invention of the telephone was a hundred years ago. It might take us as far beyond speech as speech took us beyond grunts. Groups of human brains might be able to work together with parallel channels generating intellectual creations and insights far beyond what any one of them could do individually—a thing almost impossible with our verbal single-channel bottleneck in interpersonal communication today. The full possibilities may not even be expressible in our language of verbal communication, any more than the full potentialities of verbal communication could have been expressed in the preverbal language of grunts.

Reshaping biology.—If we can arrive at a world structure based on confident planning and growth, with a good share of the world's budget devoted to education and science, many other biological possibilities will begin to be explored. The systematic farming of the oceans, the setting up of wildlife preserves, and the control of pollution seem to be almost inevitable trends today, held back only by the present disagreements between nations. The shaping of new plants and animals for various environments, perhaps with chromosome transplants to yield interspecies hybrids with new characteristics, will become big business. Control of the development of animals so as to make muscles, bones, or brains larger or more specialized may become an important study. It may be coupled with the intensive education and conditioning of animals to give them novel skills, so that they will become more intelligent and valuable as work animals or pets.

With all this, it still seems that human development by the manipulation of human genetics, except to correct acknowledged diseases and disorders, may be postponed for awhile. Someday there might be genetic copying of brilliant or talented persons so that their chromosome combinations will not be lost; tissue samples for this purpose could be stored in tissue banks for ·a long time to come. The business of restructuring education, development, and the food supply and of getting used to the new freedoms and prospects may be so absorbing that the further manipulation of human genetics could be delayed until we have a better understanding of what we are doing.

Nevertheless, sometime in the future there will almost certainly be a general demand to explore some of the possible variations in the human and protoplasmic potentiality—just as an individual today might explore and develop his various talents one after another. When that time comes, there will surely be attempts to make different parts of the brain larger or more complex, so as to make more talented musicians or poets, or more lithe and graceful people, or more talented and sensitive workers with others. It seems almost inevitable that our children of the generations ahead will try to express, by means of specialization, whatever their value systems have come to esteem at the time, even if it means a different trial arrangement of the bodily organs or the hands or eyes or brain.

Is this a reprehensible or dangerous thing? Yes, for men playing carelessly or selfishly or stupidly. Yes, for Dr. Frankenstein and Dr. Moreau. But in the long run it is surely not reprehensible for men going into it with choice and preparation and love for the potentialities of man, and with society's knowledge and approval and society's care for the creatures that are not successful.

Is this not what biology has been doing all the time, for billions of years—expanding the brain and changing our posture and limbs? Since some 6 percent of all children born today have observable genetic defects, we know that biology's experiments are still going on. But men have now become the hands of evolution. We have reached the stage where it is time for design instead of happenings by death and accident, and where it is time for anticipation and planning of what new varieties of men can do and how they will work together, instead of leaving it only to the yearning and primitive methods of the choice of a pretty partner and of learning by survival.

In addition, of course, the mechanical robots and automata of the next generation will become ever more sophisticated. A few men are already trying to make something like a learning nervous system, "grown" chemically from millions of solid-state crystals with their filaments making new contacts as various input patterns of electrical impulses flow through them. If such a system is ever successful, with parallel processing a million times faster than ours, it might be able to absorb a lifetime of experiences in an hour and go through ten million years of evolution of brain and control circuits in ten years.

Today one can think of dozens of complex problems for such electronic brains to solve and to explain to us. Conceivably the most interesting part of life could come to be the interaction with such perceiving-learning-knowing devices that could solve our problems so much faster than we can. Some scientists and managers today may already feel that way about their data banks and computers. For, as Hoyle has implied, it is not true that the only ways to interact successfully with a corner of the universe are the ways of the primitive DNA. It is not true that the only way to make a plastic learning intelligence that studies and understands the universe is with protoplasm and biological cells and neurons. Marvelous as they are to us, in some deep sense all these may be only primitive stages in the evolution of faster and more complex intelligences.

Intelligence is the universe understanding and shaping itself. Is there any reason why it must be limited to our beloved protoplasm? This has not been said clearly except by science fiction, but all our lives today are the science fiction of yesterday. It seems that we are approaching the time when we must look at these possibilities seriously and without embarrassment. We must see which of them are only fiction and which are prophecy, expressing the deep demands of our own evolutionary development and the pressures of the great evolutionary process in which we are caught up, moving on from stage to stage—the process of the universe learning to understand itself. Is that so frightening? We are at the threshold, if we survive, of an organism integrated and clear-eyed about fearlessly shaping its future development, in whatever form and complex combination of enzymes, crystals, and electrons it chooses.

WORLD STRUCTURES

What will be the structural form, the social and organizational form of this organism, man? The kind of society that lies ahead obviously depends, in a most uncertain way, on the nature of the peace-keeping solutions we happen to arrive at, by design or accident, in the next few years, if we survive. Will there simply be an indefinite continuation of the partition of the world between nuclear superpowers, held in partial check by tacit decision rules? Probably not, because this is inherently unstable, as we have seen, and will soon lead either to nuclear holocaust or to the adoption of some safer international structure.

Will there be unchecked population growth everywhere until

the whole world becomes a crowded starving Indian village? Probably not, because the problem of international structure will have been solved in some way before the population problem becomes absolutely uncontrollable. And an effective world organization will almost certainly be interested in economic growth and well-being and will have ample incentives and means, as we have seen, to control population growth.

Will there be a world dictatorship under some strong man who pulls off a fantastically dangerous bluff at a critical moment? Possibly, but the managerial characteristics of advanced governments make dictatorship increasingly more difficult. Conversely, a world dictatorship, if one were established, would be likely to become increasingly run by committees. Managerial or committee lock-ins, of course, might be terrifyingly rigid and oppressive. But the whole pressure of industrial technology in the twentieth century has been away from dictatorship and slavery and toward machines with well-paid designers, with more well-being, education, and freedom for the whole population. These are the most profitable directions of development, even for the managers.

This means that there are still some grounds for hope. In spite of our escalating hostilities, there are signs of stalemate and restraint, and, with continuing efforts toward peacemaking, the world might live to see a gradual extension of nuclear agreements, perhaps with an intermittent extension of the effectiveness of the United Nations, or else a world convention to design a more effective and more stable peace-keeping structure. From the point of view of systems theory, considerations of this kind are not politics but collective biology, more important to the health of man than his food supply. The essential point is that the only possibilities that are viable in the long run are those in which man reaches control of the planet and of his social conflicts and adopts a peace-keeping system that will really hold the organism together for at least the next few hundred years.

The last thirty years have given us more tested experimental knowledge about the biological, psychological, and social nature of man, his origin, powers, and potentialities, than everything that was known before. It is time to integrate this new knowledge into a picture of man on which future societies—good self-maintaining societies—can be based.

What we find is partly what has always been known, that man is a creature of paradoxes. He is a body, but he is also a brain, with curiosity, intelligence, and high complexity. He has been made out of dust, but now he uses the energies of the sun itself. He has been created through evolution, but now he is the principal creator of evolution.

And though man is an individual, he is also a social creature. His intelligence is within a shell of bone, but it interacts with other intelligences and changes the world. He shapes his cultures, and then his cultures shape him. By early training, he can be made arrogant or cooperative, creative or stultified. Yet, however carefully he is taught or conditioned, his quest for variety sets him exploring new patterns.

Man can be studied as an object, but he is also a communicating co-subject who wants to be treated as a person and to help plan the study. His cultures are shaped by collective forces, and yet they can be transformed by a single leader or inventor. He can organize trillion-dollar societies, and yet he stands on a knife-edge of his own making between a vista of abundance and the blackest of eternities.

What would a good society be for such a creature of search and tension? Obviously it could never be a society in which the tension would be gone. How dull! Men would gamble their lives on new forms of daring, new political demands, new art, music, and philosophy, just to make it interesting again. Creative tensions pull the cart of growth. In a good society the diversity, tension, and dialogue would never be stopped except by the danger of mutual annihilation of men, their work, or ideas. What an education! We are already plunged into it now.

A creative and evolving society will be continually driven by the gap and tension between what is and the ever-changing realization of what might be. This is the error-signal that feeds back to stimulate men's ambitions and energies and leads them to new jobs, new inventions, and new movements. In fact, it might be said that the gap between what is and what might be is the "potential energy" that drives all the wheels of society, the only real source of power in the world. Yes, it is a force that is often blocked by habit or social friction or turned into personal profit by men filling a private energy gap of their own, but it presses steadily through classes and nations, breaking up the logjams and recreating the structures until men begin to be satisfied that their hopes and dreams are being met with all reasonable speed.

To turn this energy into real advances, an immense amount of social planning will be needed. Nevertheless, a well-educated society will continually resist being dominated or manipulated by planning elites. This is the message of the unrest in the world today, and the reason for the demand for "participatory democracy," in the schools, in the ghettos, and in the Third World nations. We are free and independent persons, and we want to be taught rather than ordered, persuaded rather than commanded, bargained with rather than bombed. A good definition of poverty is the inability to command events that affect one's life. This defines financial poverty and political, intellectual, and spiritual poverty; and well-educated men will demand to be poor no more.

We therefore discover something deeper than democracy—that we are co-subjects in the choosing network—so that from now on what is done must be done not by "social engineering" but by "social cooperation." Over the long run, the intellectual or leader will be successful only if he leads, only if he is not a dictator but a counselor, not the sole designer of the system but the seer and explainer of the consequences of doing things one way rather than another. But when leaders and followers alike come to feel that their effort is mutual and that society's goals are their goals, they will cooperate in vast and difficult projects and be willing to go through fire and death. By sharing in the design, they become willing to accept their part in whatever sacrifice is needed.

The new rights.—A society is but the needs and feedbacks of the individual projected onto the social sky. It becomes unstable if its lock-ins continue to deny for very long some important part of a man's conception of himself as a person and a participant. The result is that every age must meet the developing threats and aspirations of the time by redefining the rights and duties of the individual. In one age this requires a Magna Carta; in another, religious tolerance; in another, freedom of speech and of the press; in another, equality of the vote; in another, the rights of women. The present times and those just ahead will be times of increasing crowding, increasing planning on a larger scale, and increasing loss of privacy, from other individuals, from scientific research, and from government agencies. New definitions and new customs will be needed if life is to be tolerable and if the individual is to continue to be able to choose his own values and ways of life, as well-educated men will want to.

One of our new rights should be the right to idiosyncrasy. Our lives would be happier, less guilty, and more interesting if we had the same tolerance of idiosyncrasy as of religion. Each of us needs the right to be fat or thin, to sleep when sleepy, and to work at odd hours, to have more diversity of speech, dress, and action, without criticism or group pressure. In fact, it cannot be long before we discover that the pressures of our cities and traffic jams will greatly decrease if we work and play around the clock and around the week and take vacations around the year.

We also need to enlarge the rights of children. This is not only for the children's sake but because rejected and undereducated children are expensive to society for the rest of their lives. Every child deserves, and will surely achieve, the rights he would have as a member of a rich man's family. These include the right to be wanted when born, the right to be educated up to his full potentiality and given the best wisdom of society, the right not to be lied to, not to be treated as an object, and the more subtle rights of humor and play and time to be alone and think.

We need to enlarge the rights of adults. In an affluent society, the first right is the right to share in the wealth of the world—like a rich man's sons—regardless of accidents of birth. Any society that blocks this possibility is in perpetual danger. The right to the real wealth of the world includes the right to food, shelter, education, communication, and transport, the right to space, beauty, vacations, and diversity, the right not to be punished for unavoidable accidents, the right to sex, even in prisons and asylums, and the right to have children without being overcrowded by other men's children.

Each of us also needs the right not to be treated as an object. If we are to avoid alienation, we need to participate in the full truth and depth of what life is. We need to treat each other, and to be treated, as co-subjects, as participants and persons. This means something like the right not to be lied to by doctors and officials, or betrayed by counselors, the right not to be manipulated or deceived for scientific experiments, the right to have grievances heard responsibily and rectified, the right to get information and to travel and see, the right of the generations neither to be separated nor to be pushed together, the right not to be overanesthetized, and the right to an easy death.

Some of these new rights will involve the loss of old financial and family rights, just as democracy involved the loss of feudal rights. They will demand a new personal accountability, with the loss, for example, of the right of running away and perhaps also of the right of secrecy in transactions (as represented already by the openness of public books and the new Public Information Law). They will certainly mean the loss of the right to have any number of children or to educate them to superstition or delinquency— rights which even John Stuart Mill said parents should not have.

And they will mean a new accountability and a new demand for credibility of all in authority—a demand which is growing already today.

The eternal options.—The idea of an exactly determined and predictable future—the "myth of frozen passage"—is only a myth, even in physics and philosophy, as we have noted earlier. Although we have been brought to *this* point on the path, and our values and preferences have been shaped, by forces in evolution and in ourselves and our society that are no longer within our control, we see that now; we have learned something; and our choice of the next step of the path is always open-ended. It is open-ended for the individual and for the society, because an amplifying decision-system shapes and manipulates its environment and itself by its own rules which it makes up as it goes along.

The future is unpredictable because the freedom of man makes him unpredictable. He is continually open to change, adapting and creating at rates we should not have believed possible before this generation. The result is that one generation's morality may be the next generation's anathema. One generation's brilliant design may be the next generation's black refusal. It is a collective existentialism, in which the world is decided on afresh at every moment, and where no one, neither the fathers nor the books nor God nor a theory of what is best, makes the rules for us except as we choose them freely anew at every moment.

Every generation from now on will face something like the same existential and immediate choice we face—the option of suicide or of freedom with effort, cooperation, and abundance. We can set up structures to help our children keep from killing themselves by accident and to give them time to think what they are doing, but we cannot force them to keep these structures and we cannot finally determine their values. We can only demonstrate our own values in the structures we build for them and then acknowledge that the future is open-ended, to be chosen afresh by new men every morning.

It is this change from drift to choice, to collective responsibility and commitment, that dominates all the other changes today. It is the change from the adolescent to the man. It is the change from evolution by ignorance and fatal acceptance to evolution by intelligence, anticipation, and decision. It is the change from being run by aristocrats or capitalists or managers to participatory democracy. We have bitten into the apple of knowledge and our eyes are opened. We have been driven out of the Eden of irresponsibility into the world of decision. We now know that it is we who are responsible for shaping the future. Whether we live or die, we will never be able to go back to irresponsibility again.

VII

What We Must Do

A large-scale mobilization of scientists may be the only way to solve our crisis problems of the next few years.

THERE IS ONLY ONE CRISIS in the world. It is the crisis of transformation. The trouble is that it is now coming upon us as a storm of crises from every direction. To understand why this is happening and what we must do about it, we need to understand the technological changes that have brought us to this point.

The essence of the matter is that we are on a steeply-rising 'S-curve' of change. We are undergoing a great historical transition to new levels of technological power all over the world. We all know about these changes, but we do not often stop to realize how large they are in orders of magnitude, or how vast compared to all previous changes in history. In the last century, we have increased our speeds of communication by a factor of 10^7; our speeds of travel by 10^2; our speeds of computers by 10^6; our energy resources by 10^3; our ability to control diseases by something like 10^2; and our rate of population growth to 10^3 times what it was a few thousand years ago.

Could anyone suppose that human relations around the world would not be affected to their very roots by such changes? Within just the last twenty-five years, the Western world has moved into an age of jet planes, missiles and satellites, nuclear power and nuclear terror. We have acquired computers and automation, a service and leisure economy, superhighways, superagriculture, supermedicine, mass higher education, universal TV, oral contraceptives, environmental pollution and urban crises. The rest of the world is also moving rapidly and may catch up with all these powers and problems within a very short time. It is hardly surprising that young people under thirty, who have grown up familiar with these things from childhood, have developed very different expectations and concerns from the older generation that grew up in another world.

What many people do not realize is that many of these technological changes are now approaching certain natural limits. The 'S-
curve' is beginning to level off. We may never have faster communications or more TV or larger weapons or a higher level of danger
than we have now. This means that if we could learn how to manage these new powers and problems in the next few years without
killing ourselves by our obsolete structures and behavior, we might
be able to create new and more effective social structures that
would last for many generations. We might be able to move into
that new world of abundance and diversity and well-being for all
mankind which technology has now made possible.

The trouble is that we may not survive these next few years.
The human race today is like a rocket on a launching pad. We
have been building up to this moment of take-off for a long time,
and if we can get safely through the take-off period, we may fly on a
new and exciting course for a long time to come. But at this moment, as the powerful new engines are fired, their thrust and roar
shakes and stresses every part of the ship and may cause the whole
thing to blow up before we can steer it on its way. Our problem
today is to harness and direct these tremendous new forces through
this dangerous transition period to the new world instead of to destruction. But unless we can do this, the rapidly increasing strains
and crises of the next decade may kill us all. They will make the
last 20 years look like a peaceful interlude.

THE NEXT TEN YEARS

Several types of crisis may reach explosion-point in the next ten
years: nuclear escalation, famine, participatory crises, race crises,
and what have been called the crises of administrative "legitimacy."
It is worth singling out two or three of these to see how imminent
and dangerous they are, so that we can fully realize how very little
time we have for preventing or controlling them.

Take the problem of nuclear war, for example. A few years
ago, Leo Szilard estimated the "half-life" of the human race with respect to nuclear escalation as being between ten and twenty years.
His reasoning then is still valid now. As long as we continue to
have no adequate stabilizing peace-keeping structures for the world,
we continue to live under the daily threat not only of local wars but
of nuclear escalation with overkill and megatonnage enough to destroy all life on earth. Every year or two there is a confrontation between nuclear powers—Korea, Laos, Berlin, Suez, Quemoy, Cuba,

Vietnam, and the rest. MacArthur wanted to use nuclear weapons in Korea, and in the Cuban missile crisis, John Kennedy is said to have estimated the probability of a nuclear exchange as about 25 percent.

The danger is not so much that of the unexpected, such as a radar error or even a new nuclear dictator, as it is that our present systems will work exactly as planned!—from border testing and strategic gambles and threat and counter-threat, all the way up to that 'second-strike capability' that is already aimed, armed and triggered to wipe out hundreds of millions of people in a three-hour duel!

What is the probability of this in the average incident? 10 percent? 5 percent? There is no average incident. But it is easy to see that five or ten more such confrontations in this game of 'nuclear roulette' might indeed give us only a 50–50 chance of living until 1980 or 1990. This is a shorter life expectation than people have ever had in the world before. All our medical increases in length of life are meaningless, as long as our nuclear lifetime is so short.

Many agricultural experts also think that within this next decade the great famines will begin, with deaths that may reach one hundred million people in densely populated countries like India and China. There are some who contradict this, claiming that the remarkable new grains and new agricultural methods introduced in the last three years in Southeast Asia may now be able to keep the food supply ahead of population growth. But others think that the reeducation of farmers and consumers to use the new grains cannot proceed fast enough to make a difference.

But if famine does come, it is clear that it will be catastrophic. Besides the direct human suffering, it will further increase our international instabilities, with food riots, troops called out, governments falling, and international interventions that will change the whole political map of the world. It could make Vietnam look like a popgun.

In addition, the next decade is likely to see continued crises of legitimacy of all our overloaded and surprised administrations, from universities and unions to cities and national governments. The problem is not peculiar to America or to capitalist countries, as we can tell by looking at student revolutions around the globe. It is not a matter of rich or poor, or of Left or Right, in the old sense. We find the suburbs marching against school "busing" at the same instant that the ghettos are marching against slum clearance plans.

In spite of the violence of some of these confrontations, this may seem like a trivial problem compared to war or famine—until we realize the dangerous effects of these instabilities on the stability of the whole system. A high-information society now insists on being consulted and not commanded. This is reasonable enough, but it puts a fresh burden on administrations already faced with mounting responsibilities and new puzzles that no one yet knows how to handle. Traditional methods of election and management do not give them the speed, capacity and knowledge needed for these new problems. They become swollen, incompetent, unresponsive—and vulnerable. Every day now some distinguished leader is pressured out of office by protesting constituents.

This in turn makes the nuclear crisis and all the other crises more dangerous—because administrators or mediators today may often work out a basis of agreement between conflicting groups or nations, only to find themselves repudiated by their people on one or both sides, who are then left with no mechanism except to escalate their battles further.

THE CRISIS OF CRISES

What finally makes all of our crises still more dangerous is that they are now coming on top of each other. Most administrations are able to endure or even enjoy an occasional crisis, with everyone working late together and getting a new sense of importance and unity. What they are not prepared to deal with is multiple crises, a crisis of crises all at one time. This is what happened in New York City in 1968 when there was the Ocean Hill-Brownsville teacher and race strike on top of a police strike, on top of a garbage strike, on top of a longshoremen's strike, all within a few days of each other.

When something like this happens, the staffs get jumpy with smoke and coffee and alcohol, the mediators become exhausted, and the administrators find themselves running two crises behind. Every problem may escalate because those involved no longer have time to think straight. What would have happened in the Cuban missile crisis if the East Coast power blackout had occurred by accident that same day? Or if the "hot line" between Washington and Moscow had gone dead? There might have been hours of misinterpretation, and some fatally different decisions.

I think this multiplication of domestic and international crises today will shorten that short half-life. In the continued absence of better ways of heading off these multiple crises, our half-life may no longer be ten to twenty years, but more like five to ten years, or less. We may have even less than a 50–50 chance of living until 1980.

This statement may seen uncertain and excessively dramatic. But is there any scientist who would make a much more optimistic estimate after considering all the different sources of danger and how they are increasing? The shortness of the time is due to the exponential and multiplying character of our problems and not to what particular numbers or guesses we put in. Anyone who feels more hopeful about getting past the demons of the 1970s has only to look beyond them to the giants of pollution and population rising up in the 1980s and 1990s. Whether we have ten years or more like twenty or thirty, unless we systematically find new large-scale solutions, we are in the gravest danger of destroying our society, our world, and ourselves in any of a number of different ways well before the end of the century. Our futurologists who predict what the world will be like in the year 2000 have neglected to tell us that.

But the real reason for trying to make a rational estimate of these deadlines is not because of their shock value but because they give us a rough idea of how much time we may have for finding and mounting some large-scale solutions. The time is short but, as we shall see, it is not too short to give us a chance that something can be done, if we begin immediately.

From this point, there is no place to go but up. In human affairs, there is no such thing as an absolute prediction or an absolute future, but only a conditional future which depends on what we do and can be made worse or better by stupid or intelligent action. To change our earlier analogy, today we are like men in a dark tunnel in a coal mine who can hear the rock rumbling already, but who can also see a little square of light at the end of the tunnel. Against this background, I am an optimist—in that I want to insist that there is a square of light and that it is worth trying to get to. I think what we must do is to start running as fast as possible toward that light, working to increase the probability of our survival through this decade by some measurable amount.

For the light at the end of the tunnel is very bright indeed. If we can only devise new mechanisms to help us survive this round of terrible crises, we have a chance of moving into a new world of incredible potentialities for all mankind. But if we cannot get through this next decade, we may never reach it.

TASK FORCES FOR SOCIAL RESEARCH AND DEVELOPMENT

What can we do? I think the problem before us requires something very similar to the mobilization of scientists for solving crisis problems in wartime. Nothing less than the application of the full intelligence of our society is likely to be adequate. I think we are going to need large numbers of scientists forming something like research teams, or Task Forces, for Social Research and Development. We need full-time interdisciplinary teams, including natural scientists, social scientists, doctors, engineers, teachers, lawyers, and many other trained and inventive minds, who will put together our stores of knowledge and powerful new ideas into action-oriented, policy-directed 'social inventions' that will have a chance of being adopted soon enough and widely enough to be effective. Even a great mobilization of scientists may not be enough. There is no guarantee that these problems can be solved, or solved in time, no matter what we do. But for problems of this scale and urgency, it is the only chance we have.

Scientists, of course, are not the only ones who can make contributions. Millions of citizens, business and labor leaders, city and government officials, and workers in existing agencies, are already doing all they can to solve these problems. No scientific innovation will be effective without extensive advice and help from all these groups.

But it is the new science and technology that have made our problems so immense and intractable. Technology did not create human conflicts and inequities, but it has made them unendurable. And where science and technology have expanded the problems in this way, it may only be more scientific understanding and better technology that can carry us past them. The cure for the pollution of the rivers by detergents is nonpolluting detergents. The cure for bad management designs is better management designs.

Moreover, in many areas, there are few people outside the research community who have the basic knowledge necessary for radically new solutions. In our biological problems, the new ideas from biochemistry and ecology may be crucial. In our social-organizational problems, it may be the new theories of organization and management and behavior theory and game theory that offer the only hope. Scientific Task Forces may be the only way in which many of these new ideas can be converted into practical invention and action.

The time scale that such Task Forces would have to work on is very different from what is usual in science. In the past, most scientists have tended to work on something like a thirty-year time scale, hoping that their careful studies would fit into some great intellectual synthesis that might be years away. Of course when they become politically concerned, they begin to work on something more like a three-month time scale, collecting signatures or trying to persuade the government to start or stop some program.

But thirty years is too long, and three months is too short, for the urgency and dimensions of these crises that might destroy us in the next 10 years. Our urgent problems now are more like wartime problems, where we need to work as rapidly as is consistent with large-scale effectiveness. For such work, what is needed is more like a three-year time scale—or more broadly, a one-to-five-year time scale. In World War II, the ten thousand scientists who were mobilized for war research knew they did not have thirty years, or ten

TABLE 1

CLASSIFICATION OF PROBLEMS AND CRISES BY ESTIMATED TIME AND INTENSITY (U.S.)

Grade	*Estimated Crisis Intensity* (number affected times degree of effect)	*Estimated Time to Crisis* (if no major effort at anticipatory solution)		
		1–5 Years	5–20 Years	20–50 Years
1.	*Total Annihilation*	*Nuclear or RCBW Escalation*	*Nuclear or RCBW Escalation*	✠ (Solved or dead)
2.	10^8 *Great Destruction or Change* (*Physical, Biological, or Political*)	(too soon)	Participatory Democracy Eco-balance	Political Theory and Economic Structure Population Planning Patterns of Living Education Communications Integrative Philosophy
3.	10^7 *Widespread Almost Unbearable Tension*	Administrative Management Slums Participatory Democracy Race Conflict	Pollution Poverty Law and Justice	?
4.	10^6 *Large-Scale Distress*	Transportation Neighborhood Ugliness Crime	Communications-Gaps	?

Grade	Estimated Crisis Intensity (number affected times degree of effect)	Estimated Time to Crisis (if no major effort at anticipatory solution) →		
		1–5 Years	5–20 Years	20–50 Years
5.	10^5 *Tension Producing Responsive Change*	Cancer and Heart Smoking and Drugs Artificial Organs Accidents Sonic Boom Water Supply Marine Resources Privacy on computers	Educational Inadequacy	?
6.	*Other Problems —Important, but Adequately Researched*	Military R&D New Educational Methods Mental Illness Fusion Power	Military R&D	
7.	*Exaggerated Dangers and Hopes*	Mind Control Heart Transplants Definition of Death	Sperm Banks Freezing Bodies Unemployment from Automation	Eugenics
8.	*Non-Crisis Problems Being "Overstudied"*	Man in Space *Most Basic Science*		

years, to come up with answers. But they did have time for the new research, design and construction that brought sonar and radar and atomic energy to operational effectiveness within one to four years. Today we need the same large-scale mobilization for innovation and action and the same sense of constructive urgency.

PRIORITIES: A CRISIS INTENSITY CHART

It is most important to be clear about which problems are the real priority problems in such an enterprise. To get this straight, it is valuable to try to separate the different problems according to some measures of their scale and urgency. A possible classification of this kind is shown in Tables 1 and 2. In these tables, I have tried to

TABLE 2

CLASSIFICATION OF PROBLEMS AND CRISES BY ESTIMATED TIME AND INTENSITY (WORLD)

Grade	Estimated Crisis Intensity (number affected times degree of effect)	Estimated Time to Crisis (if no major effort at anticipatory solution)		
		1–5 Years	5–20 Years	20–50 Years
1.	10^{10} *Total Annihilation*	*Nuclear or RCBW Escalation*	*Nuclear or RCBW Escalation*	✛ (Solved or dead)
2.	10^9 *Great Destruction or Change* (*Physical, Biological,* or *Political*)	(too soon)	Famines Eco-balance Development Failures Local Wars Rich-Poor Gap	Economic Structure and Political Theory Population and Eco-balance Patterns of Living Universal Education Communications-Integration Management of World Integrative Philosophy
3.	10^8 *Widespread Almost Unbearable Tension*	Administrative Management Need for Participation Group and Race Conflict Poverty-Rising Expectations Environmental Degradation	Poverty Pollution Race Wars Political Rigidity Strong Dictatorships	?
4.	10^7 *Large-Scale Distress*	Transportation Diseases Loss of old cultures	Housing Education Independence of Big Powers Communications Gap	?

Grade	Estimated Crisis Intensity (number affected times degree of effect)	Estimated Time to Crisis (if no major effort at anticipatory solution)		
		1–5 Years	5–20 Years	20–50 Years
5.	10^6 *Tension Producing Responsive Change*	Regional Organization Water Supplies	?	?
6.	*Other Problems —Important, but Adequately Researched*	Technical Development Design Intelligent Monetary Design		
7.	*Exaggerated Dangers and Hopes*			Eugenics Melting of Ice Caps
8.	*Non-Crisis Problems Being "Overstudied"*	Man in Space *Most Basic Science*		

rank a number of present or potential problems or crises, vertically, according to an estimate of their order of intensity or "seriousness"; and horizontally, by a rough estimate of their time to reach climactic importance. Table 1 is such a classification for the United States for the next 1–5 years, the next 5–20 years, and the next 20–50 years. Table 2 is a similar classification for world problems and crises.

The successive rows indicate something like order-of-magnitude differences in crisis intensity, as estimated by a rough product of the size of population that might be hurt or affected, times some estimated average effect in the disruption of their lives. Thus the top row corresponds to total or near-total annihilation, the second row to great destruction or change affecting everybody, the third row to a lower tension affecting a smaller part of the population or a smaller part of everyone's life, and so on.

Informed men might easily disagree about one row up or down in intensity, or one column left or right in the time-scales, but these order-of-magnitude differences are already so great that it would be surprising to find much larger disagreements. Clearly an important initial step in any serious problem study would be to refine such estimates.

In both Tables, the one crisis that must be ranked at the top in total danger and imminence is, of course, the danger of large-scale or total annihilation by nuclear escalation or by radiological-chemical-biological-warfare (RCBW). The crisis continues through the 1–5 year period and the 5–20 year period as Crisis Number 1, unless and until we get a safer peace-keeping arrangement. But in the 20–50 year column, I think we must simply put a big "X" at this level, on the grounds that this problem will either be solved by that time or we will probably be dead.

At the second level, the 1–5 year period may not be a period of great destruction (except nuclear) in either the United States or the world. But the problems at this level are building up. Many scientists fear the destruction of our ecological balance in the United States by mismanagement or pollution in the 5–20 year period; others now fear great political damage from participatory confrontations, by backlash or dictatorship, if these problems are not solved before that time.

On a world scale in this period, famine and ecological catastrophe head the list of destructive problems. We will come back later to the items in the 20–50 year column.

The third level of crisis problems in the United States includes the problems that are already upon us: administrative management of communities and cities, slums, participatory democracy, and race conflict. In the 5–20 year period, the problems of pollution and poverty or major failures of law and justice could escalate to this level of tension if they are not solved. The last column is left blank because secondary events and second-order effects will interfere seriously with any attempt to make longer-range predictions at these lower levels.

The rest of the items in both tables need not be discussed here in detail. Some are common headline problems which are included to show how they might rank quantitatively in this kind of comparison. Anyone concerned with any of them will find it a useful exercise to estimate for himself their order of seriousness, in terms of the number of people they actually affect and the average distress they cause. Transportation problems and neighborhood ugliness, for example, are listed as Grade 4 problems in the United States because they depress the lives of tens of millions for one or two hours every day. Violent crime may affect a corresponding number every year or two. These evils are not negligible, and they are worth the efforts of enormous numbers of people to cure them and to keep them cured —but they will not destroy our society either.

The Grade 5 crises are those where the hue and cry has been raised and where responsive changes of some kind are already underway. Cancer goes here, along with problems like auto safety and an adequate water supply. This does not mean that we have solved the problem of cancer—we may never solve it!—but that good people are working on it and are making as much progress as we could expect from anyone. (At this level of concern, a more elaborate chart might also begin to list things which are not problems but neglected opportunities, such as the automation of clinical biochemistry or the invention of new channels of personal communication, which could affect the 20-year future as greatly as automobiles and telephones have affected the present.)

Where The Scientists Are

Below Grade 5, three less quantitative categories are listed, where the scientists begin to outnumber the problems. Grade 6 consists of problems that are important but are "adequately researched" at the present time. Military research and development belongs in this category. It is certainly important in our present world of nation-states, but it engrosses hundreds of thousands of scientists and engineers, and it is being taken care of adequately and generously. Likewise fusion power, interesting as it may be, is being studied at the hundred-million-dollar level, but if we had it tomorrow, it would scarcely change our rates of application of nuclear energy to the power problem of the world.

Grade 7 contains the "exaggerated problems" which are being talked about or worked on out of all proportion to their true importance, such as heart transplants, which can never affect more than a few thousands of people out of the billions in the world. It is sad to note that the symposia on "social implications of science" at many national scientific meetings are often on the problems of Grade 7.

In the last category, Grade 8, are two subjects which I am sorry to say I must call "overstudied." By this I mean that they are overstudied with respect to the real crisis problems today. The Man in Space flights to the moon and back are the most beautiful technical achievements of man, but they are not urgent except for national display, and they absorb tens of thousands of our most ingenious technical brains.

And in the "overstudied" list I think I must also put most basic science. There are some studies that are immediately relevant to our human problems further up the scale, but for every one of these I think there may be a dozen others exploring tinier and tinier corners of knowledge or repeating the same kind of studies over and over again on the next thousand molecules. Students as well as researchers are beginning to feel this lack of real importance in many of our studies in every field. There are a host of scientific problems that we could postpone for fifty years if we had to, without any great loss.

Long-range science is useless unless we survive to use it. For all the beauty and long-term value of basic science, when we see the scale and urgency of our world-wide problems today, the idea of "science as usual" is so irrelevant and wasteful of tens of thousands of our best scientific minds that it approaches frivolity.

The diagonal arrows in the tables are intended to indicate that problems that are not solved at one level may escalate upward to a higher level of crisis in the next time period. The arrows toward Level 2 in the last columns of both Tables show the escalation of all our problems upward to some general reconstruction in the 20–50 year time period, if we survive. Probably no human institution will survive unchanged for another fifty years, because they will be changed by the crises if they are not changed in advance to prevent them. There will surely be widespread changes in all our ways of life everywhere, from our political theory and economic structure and patterns of living to our whole philosophy of man. But whether the world will resemble an open humanist democracy based on technical abundance with coexistence of numerous diverse forms, or something more like Orwell's *1984*—or a crippled society in a post-nuclear desert with its scientists hanged—is something that our acts of commitment and leadership in the next few years will decide.

MOBILIZING SCIENTISTS

It is a unique experience for us to have peace-time problems, or technical problems which are not industrial problems, on such a scale. We do not know quite where to start, and there is no mechanism yet for generating ideas systematically or paying teams to turn them into successful solutions.

But the years ahead may be like a war in which the main enemies are our own ignorance and confusion about what to do for the good of us all. I think the anti-submarine warfare work in 1940 or the Manhattan Project on atomic energy may be the closest parallels to what we must do in terms of novelty and scale and urgency, and the methods of mobilization and the success to be achieved. In the anti-submarine campaign, Blackett assembled miscellaneous scientists and other clever minds in his "back room," and within a few months they had worked out the "operations analysis" that made an order-of-magnitude difference in the success of the operation. In the atomic energy work, scientists started out by spending nights and weekends on the new problem. They formed a central committee to channel their secret communications and then, after they had begun to see the dimensions of the problem, they went to the government for large-scale support which led to the setting up of the great laboratories and production plants.

Fortunately, work on our crisis problems today would not require secrecy. Scientists from many countries who know that these problems are already beginning to be their problems as well as ours, would have an interest in the work and might contribute important new viewpoints and ideas.

The first step today should probably be the organization of intense technical discussion and education groups in every laboratory. When it is clearer what lines are promising and interesting to a given group, they might begin systematic part-time studies, hopefully with the permission or active assistance of department heads and administrators. (Department heads and boards of directors might reflect that the survival of their own organizations is also at stake in the long run.) Coordinating committees or even new societies might be set up, and results might begin to be reported in new meetings and journals, as long as these emphasize the practical rather than the merely academic.

Several foundations and federal agencies already have in-house research and make outside grants in several of these crisis areas. Most of them would welcome additional work by top-level scientists who have not previously been involved, and they would be important initial sources for full-time support of new research and development.

But the step that will probably be required in a very short time is the creation of a new center or centers, like a new Los Alamos or Oak Ridge, or RAND of crisis studies, to bring together interdisciplinary teams of natural scientists and social scientists, doctors and engineers, team leaders and graduate students, to work full-time on these problems. "Production facilities" or training centers for full-scale dissemination of new socio-technical inventions might even be needed. Many different kinds of centers will eventually be necessary. The problems of our time—the $100-billion food problem, or the

$100-billion arms control problem—are no smaller than World War II in scale and importance, and it would be absurd to think that one or two campuses or a few agency laboratories could do the job.

The thing that discourages many scientists—even social scientists—from thinking in these research-and-development terms is their failure to realize that there are such things as social inventions and that they can have large-scale social effects in a surprisingly short time. A recent study with Karl Deutsch has examined some sixty of the great achievements in social science in this century, to see where they were made and by whom and how long they took to become effective. They include developments such as the following:

Keynesian economics
Opinion polls and statistical sampling
Input-output economics
Operations analysis
Information theory and feedback theory
Theory of games and economic behavior
Operant conditioning and programmed learning
Planned programming and budgeting (PPB)
Non-zero-sum game theory

Many of these have made remarkable differences in our ability to handle social problems or management problems within just a few years. The opinion poll became a national necessity within a single election period. The theory of games, published in 1946, had become an important component of American strategic thinking by RAND and the Defense Department by 1953, in spite of the limitation of the theory at that time to zero-sum games, with their dangerous bluffing and "brinksmanship." Today, within less than a decade, the PPB management technique is sweeping through every large organization.

This list is particularly interesting because it shows how much can be done outside official government agencies by inventive men putting their brains together. Most of the achievements were the work of teams of two or more men, almost all of them located in intellectual centers such as Princeton or the two Cambridges.

The list might be extended by adding commercial social inventions with rapid and widespread effects, like credit cards. And socio-technical inventions, like computers and automation or like oral contraceptives, which were in widespread use within a few years after they were developed. In addition, there are political innovations like the New Deal, which made great changes in our economic life within four years, and the Pay-As-You-Go Income Tax, which transformed federal taxing power within two years.

On the international scene, the Peace Corps, the "hot line," the Test-Ban Treaty, the Antarctic Treaty, and the Non-Proliferation Treaty, were all implemented within two to ten years after their initial proposal. These are only small contributions, a tiny patchwork part of the basic international stabilization system that is needed, but they show that the time to adopt good new structural designs may be surprisingly short. Our clichés about "social lag" are very misleading. Over half of the major social innovations since 1940 were adopted or had widespread social effects within less than twelve years—a time as short as, or shorter than, the average time for adoption of technological innovations.

AREAS FOR TASK FORCES

To make the case more persuasive, it may be worth listing a few areas today where Task Forces might be able to turn some of our powerful new tools or methods into practical applications with large social effects.

(1) *Biotechnology.* Humanity must feed and care for the people who are already in the world, even while we try to level off the further population explosion that makes this so difficult. We need real exploration of novel proposals for food, like the genetic copying of champion animals, or food from coal. We need to explore simpler and more effective contraceptive methods. We need teams working on recycling of wastes and low-level chemical measurements, and new inventions for measuring and maintaining the ecological balance.

(2) *Peace-keeping mechanisms and feedback stabilization.* Our various Nuclear Treaties are a beginning. But how about a technical group that sits down and thinks about the whole range of possible and impossible stabilization and peace-keeping mechanisms? Stabilization feedback-design might be a complex modern counterpart of the "checks and balances" used in designing the constitutional structure of the United States two hundred years ago. With our new knowledge today about feedbacks, group behavior, and game theory, it ought to be possible to design more complex and even more successful structures.

Some peace-keeping mechanisms that might be hard to adopt

today could nevertheless be planned and ready for a more favorable time. At some crisis moment, just before the button is pushed, there is a chance that some man or group may suddenly stop and say, "My God! What are we doing? Isn't there some other way?" And at that moment, some plan that has already been prepared and tested and publicized as well as it can be, might transform the danger into a step toward sanity. In a crisis, men fall back on familiar alternatives. In such a time, some already well-known plan might be the only chance we have.

(3) *Game theory.* Civilian task forces, as well as military and government task forces, need to work on war games and peace games and game theory. As the RAND Corporation showed, zero-sum game theory is not too academic to be used for strategy and policy. Unfortunately, in zero-sum games, what I win, you lose, and what you win, I lose. This may be the way poker works, but it is not the way the world works. We are collectively in a non-zero-sum game in which we will all lose together in a nuclear holocaust, or all win together in survival and prosperity. Some group needs to apply the many variations of non-zero-sum game theory to conflict and cooperation between individuals and groups and nations, to see if this does not bring us out in a different place from our sterile and dangerous confrontation strategies.

(4) *Behavior theory.* How could the powerful new ideas of behavior theory and the new ideas of responsive living be used to improve group and family life, and education and management and community structures? Who will apply them to the design of new types of child-care communities, and to new and more satisfying patterns of group living for the childless and the old people?

(5) *Management theory.* How could the new ideas of information handling, behavioral reinforcements, responsive management, and democratic decision-making be turned into practical recipes for reducing the daily frustrations of schools, hospitals, churches, and community organizations?

(6) *Economic theory.* Who will apply behavior theory and game theory to more satisfying bargaining? Who will devise repayment inventions that could make new Urban Development Corporations or Educational Development Corporations economically feasible? Who will finally succeed in making the systems-theory analysis of how to keep full employment from leading to inflation? Inflation pinches the poor, hurts government service, increases labor-management disputes, and multiplies all our domestic conflicts and crises and our sense of despair.

(7) *Communications.* Widespread citizens'-band radios could change traffic and crime problems and many rural and city problems. Widespread recording of personal experiences might produce important changes in our daily relationships and encounters. New publications and distribution methods could increase communication and sympathy between groups in conflict or could give us all better balanced access to national and world information.

(8) *Social indicators.* We can maximize our welfare and minimize our ills far more effectively when we can measure them accurately. We need "social indicators," like the cost-of-living index, for measuring a thousand social good and evils, such as transportation difficulties or the success of hospital management or the quality of recreation facilities. Engineers and physical scientists working with social scientists might come up with ingenious new methods of measuring many of these important but elusive parameters.

(9) *Channels of effectiveness.* We need case studies and careful analysis of the reasons for the success or failure of various social inventions. When should innovation come through planning commissions or legislation, and when should it develop from outside the Establishment? A handbook showing what methods have been successful for different large-scale social problems would be of immense value. We especially need to see what is happening to the old elite methods of centralized or behind-the-scenes planning, and what needs ·to be done so that social innovations today can obtain a wider base of participatory agreement in advance.

Such a list is merely a beginning, of course. Society is at least as complex as, say, a large automobile with its several thousand parts, and it will require at least as elaborate a development of a multitude of inventions, and inventions to improve on inventions, to solve its problems.

FUTURE SATISFACTIONS AND PRESENT SOLUTIONS

This is an enormous program. But there is nothing impossible about mounting and financing it, if we as concerned men go into it with commitment and leadership. Yes, there will be a need for money and power to overcome organizational difficulties and vested interests. But it is worth remembering that the only real source of power in the world is the gap between what is and what might be. Why else do men work and save and plan? If there is some future increase in human satisfaction that we can point to and realistically anticipate, men will be willing to pay something for it and invest in it in the hope of that return. In economics, they pay with money; in politics, with their votes and time and sometimes with their jail sentences and their lives.

Social change, peaceful or turbulent, is powered by "what might be." This means that for peaceful change, to get over some impossible barrier of unresponsiveness or complexity or group conflict, what is needed is an inventive man or group—a "social entrepreneur"—who can connect up the pieces and show how to turn the advantage of "what might be" into some present advantage for every participating party. To get toll roads, when highways were hopeless, a legislative-corporation mechanism was invented that turned the future need into present profits for construction workers and bondholders and continuing profitability for the state and all the drivers.

This principle, of broad payoff anticipatory design, was what made possible the success of the Kaiser Permanente plan for prepaid medical care, and the long-range plan that has guided Puerto Rico's remarkable development. Regular Task Forces using systems analysis to find payoffs over the barriers might give us such successful solutions much more often. In fact, the worse conditions are, the more profit there can be, economic and human, for everyone, in making them better! The new world that lies ahead, with its blocks and malfunctions removed, will be fantastically wealthy; what we are looking for is a way for intelligence to convert that large payoff into the profitable solutions of our present problems.

The only possible conclusion is a call to action. Who will commit himself to this kind of search for more ingenious and fundamental solutions? Who will begin to assemble the research teams and the funds? Who will begin to create those full-time interdisciplinary centers that will be necessary for testing detailed designs and turning them into effective applications?

The task is clear. The task is huge. The time is horribly short. In the past, we have had science for intellectual pleasure, and science for the control of nature. We have had science for war. But today, the whole human experiment may hang on how fast we now press the development of science for survival.